MERRY CHRISTMAS MOM
WE LOVE

M000247913

Wooden Hotels of Norway

LIVING LEGENDS

A journey is more than just a journey. It is anticipation, dreams, longings and experiences. It is a meeting between a person and a heritage. In Norway, it is also a journey to one of Europe's last wildernesses – untouched, wild and beautiful scenery – a journey through genuine virgin territory.

A visit to Norway's old, dignified hotels and guesthouses can be like a return to yesterday, compared with the hectic modern world. They are part of the European heritage and have retained their old-world magnificence. Generations of hotel owners have run and maintained them with a sense of tradition and pride.

These centers of accommodation are a journey back in time, before vacations were a natural part of life. They were only the privilege of royalty, the aristocracy and a few other pioneers from far flung places. Today, anyone can enter these architectural gems, close the door on the stresses of daily life and allow peace to reign in beautiful surroundings.

Welcome!

Yours sincerely,
The Norwegian Tourist Board

Dag Mork Ulnes
Man. Dir.

Wooden Hotels of Norway

LIVING LEGENDS

2nd edition 1997

Norwegian Title: Tradisjon og atmosfære
               En reise til norske trehoteller

German title: Tradition und Atmosphäre
               Die prächtigen Holzhotels in Norwegen

Publisher:
Svein Gran, KOM Forlag a/s
Vågeveien 10 6500 Kristiansund N
Norway
Phone: 47-71 67 83 00
Fax: 47-71 67 83 60

© KOM Forlag a/s

Graphic Design:
Heidi Downham, Tangen Grafiske Senter AS

Stylists:
Cecilie F. Stang and Siri Sørensen

Front page photo:
Knut Bry

Translated into
– English by Melody Favish and V. F. Stokke
– German by Lucie Fæste

Repro and printing:
Tangen Grafiske Senter AS, 1997

English edition: ISBN 82-908-2330-4
Norwegian edition: ISBN 82-908-2329-0
German edition: ISBN 82-908-2331-2

In the United States this book is distributed by:
Skandisk, Inc.
7616 Lyndale Ave S.
Minneapolis, MN 55423
Phone: 612 - 866 - 3636
Fax: 612 - 866 - 3580

Wooden Hotels of Norway

LIVING LEGENDS

Hans Martin Underdal
Jens Christian Eldal

Photos:
Rohny Kristensen, Steinar Torvbråten

KOM FORLAG

Contents

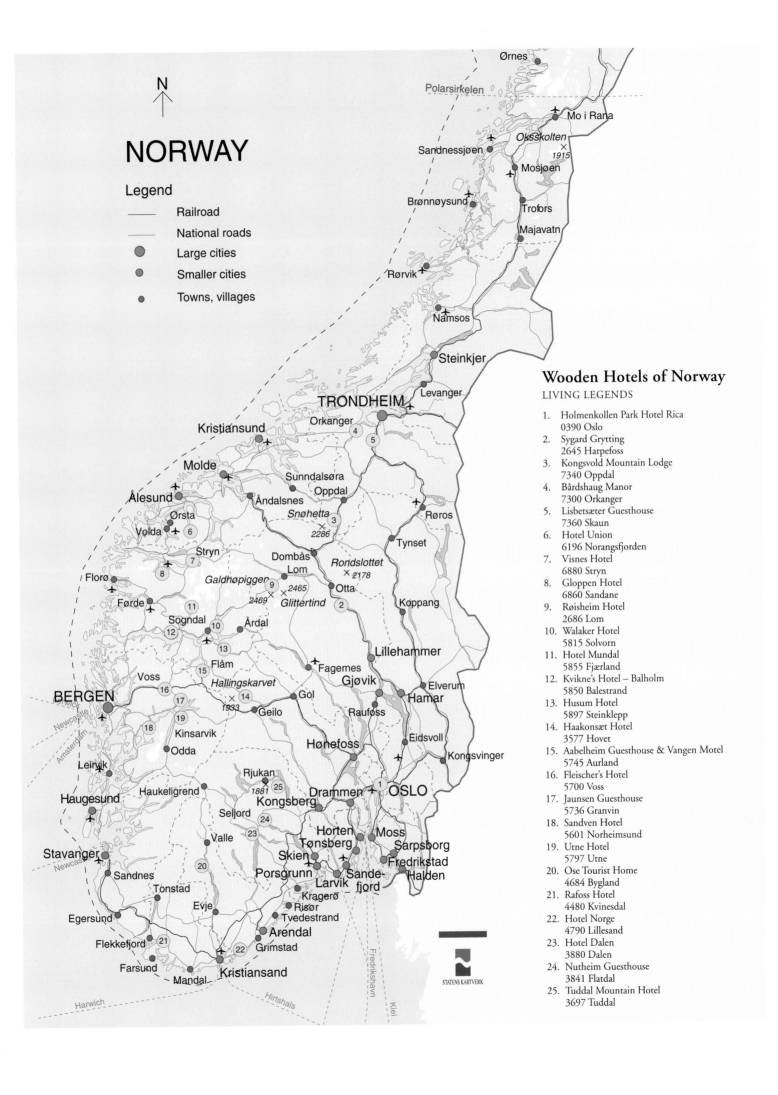

NORWAY

Legend

— Railroad
— National roads
● Large cities
● Smaller cities
• Towns, villages

Wooden Hotels of Norway

LIVING LEGENDS

1. Holmenkollen Park Hotel Rica
   0390 Oslo
2. Sygard Grytting
   2645 Harpefoss
3. Kongsvold Mountain Lodge
   7340 Oppdal
4. Bårdshaug Manor
   7300 Orkanger
5. Lisbetsæter Guesthouse
   7360 Skaun
6. Hotel Union
   6196 Norangsfjorden
7. Visnes Hotel
   6880 Stryn
8. Gloppen Hotel
   6860 Sandane
9. Røisheim Hotel
   2686 Lom
10. Walaker Hotel
    5815 Solvorn
11. Hotel Mundal
    5855 Fjærland
12. Kvikne's Hotel – Balholm
    5850 Balestrand
13. Husum Hotel
    5897 Steinklepp
14. Haakonsæt Hotel
    3577 Hovet
15. Aabelheim Guesthouse & Vangen Motel
    5745 Aurland
16. Fleischer's Hotel
    5700 Voss
17. Jaunsen Guesthouse
    5736 Granvin
18. Sandven Hotel
    5601 Norheimsund
19. Utne Hotel
    5797 Utne
20. Ose Tourist Home
    4684 Bygland
21. Rafoss Hotel
    4480 Kvinesdal
22. Hotel Norge
    4790 Lillesand
23. Hotel Dalen
    3880 Dalen
24. Nutheim Guesthouse
    3841 Flatdal
25. Tuddal Mountain Hotel
    3697 Tuddal

STATENS KARTVERK

Preface

The first tourists who came to Norway at the beginning of the 19th century were adventurers and explorers. They came in spite of poor or non-existent roads, and they "discovered" Norway on horseback and on foot.

Full of enthusiasm, they returned home and wrote descriptive travelogues about wild and powerful nature, about the fjords, the mountains, the glaciers and the waterfalls. Soon, artists, mountain climbers and salmon fishermen came. Fishing and climbing guidebooks were written and artists painted beautiful pictures of the dramatic Norwegian countryside.

Soon, Norway became an attractive and popular destination among royalty from around the world. This was duly noted, and interest increased among regular tourists. Eventually, roads and other means of communication were improved. The development of scheduled steamship traffic along the coast, as well as to England and the continent, contributed to the increase in tourists. By the end of the 19th century, the number of visitors coming to Norway had virtually exploded.

As far as accommodation was concerned, there was not much to offer these tourists. Those places to spend the night that did exist were simple inns and guesthouses. The need for good hotels was acute. Those who came to Norway demanded both comfort and luxury. That started a period of hectic building activity.

Old inns and guesthouses were expanded, and new hotels were built in central places. Today, many of the beautiful wooden hotels which were built at the end of the last century are gone. In contrast to hotels abroad, where most were built in brick or stone, Norwegian hotels were constructed of wood, the most natural building material in this country. Many of the hotels have burned down, while others have been demolished. But fortunately, some are still standing, and they have been restored in the old style.

This book presents 25 hotels in southern Norway, in which the original character has been preserved. Each place has its own special history, and together, they relate the history of the development of Norwegian tourism and of our first hotel pioneers.

Welcome to a journey to our beautiful wooden hotels, to a journey in history, tradition and atmosphere.

Oslo 1996
Hans Martin Underdal

From farmhouses to fairy tale castles

The earliest places where people could spend the night were travelers' inns. These were ordinary farms, and the architecture seldom differed from that of other farms in the district. Local building customs were the norm. There were few comforts for travelers in those days. People were satisfied just to get a bed, and a private room was a rare luxury. Cleanliness was haphazard, and there are many tales of sheepskin blankets which almost could walk on their own because of all the bedbugs. The upper classes preferred to stay at parsonages whenever they had to set out on strenuous and uncomfortable journeys, and all journeys could be described as such in the olden days.

Conditions were much better in established commercial centers and guesthouses, where separate buildings were constructed with many bedrooms for guests. Many of these have been demolished or changed to the unrecognizable, but some have been preserved intact or in pictures. Usually they were in the same style as the main buildings on the larger farms in the district, while these stylistic features, in turn, derived from either official residences or from the nearest town. Examples include Røisheim Hotel, in the Gudbrandsdal building tradition, and Kongsvold Mountain Lodge, which bears some features of the Trøndelag building tradition. Buildings in western Norway, especially those on larger farms and guesthouses, were influenced by the wooden architecture of Bergen. The finest buildings had Baroque or Neo-Classical entrances, with columns supporting pediments, as did the homes of the bourgeoisie in the cities. Utne Hotel in Hardanger features this kind of building, but it has been both altered and extended. The best preserved old building in this book is Jaunsen Guesthouse in Granvin. Other examples include Aabelheim and Wangen Motel in Aurland, where Neo-Classical portals have been preserved.

The tourist hotels, from about 1870 to 1914
Tourist traffic in Norway increased in the 1870's, even more in the 1880's and 1890's, and new types of buildings emerged – larger tourist hotels. They were built according to designs of similar tourist complexes on the continent. Switzerland was a forerunner in the construction of tourist hotels, and it is likely that many models for Norwegian tourist hotels came from there, even though the style itself was not especially Swiss. Some plans came from Germany, as well, especially from the spas with their health-giving springs, which had been resorts for many years. Seaside hotels along the coast of northwest Europe were another source of designs.

All Norwegian hotels from the last quarter of the 19th century and the beginning of the 20th century were made of wood, as opposed to stone, which was most common in other countries. Wood was, without a doubt, the cheapest building material available in Norway. In most places, materials could be obtained locally, and there were craftsmen in the district who were familiar with the local building techniques. In some places, architects were brought in from the cities, but in general, local building contractors designed, as well as built, the smaller and medium-sized hotels. Economy was a deciding factor for the architecture and the materials used. The hotels had only a short summer season, and that limited the size, standard and decoration in most places. Low hotel standards were a frequent problem, and for that reason, many felt that the wealthiest tourists were deterred from coming to Norway. But there were exceptions. Some hotels were both large and comfortable. They had their first golden age in the 25 years before World War I – the period which was called "Belle Époque."

"Swiss style" or historicism in wood
During the building boom to accommodate the rapid rise in tourism toward the end of the 19th century, there was one style which became dominant everywhere, both in hotels and in other wooden buildings. In Norwegian, it is usually called the "Swiss style." This stylistic term is often misleading, because many houses described as such do not have specifically Swiss designs. In fact, the style appears parallel to what is called the stick style, carpenter gothic or gingerbread in the United States. Important characteristics for the so-called "Swiss style" are large roof projections, verandas and ornamental gables, composed of beam constructions and jigsaw cutouts. These elements became so common in hotel architecture during the period between around 1870 and the 1920's, that it is worth investigating their role in the building style of the time.

This "Swiss style" was a result of the desire of 19th century architects to find a source among old historic buildings for a new

A typical guesthouse in western Norway from around the middle of the 1800's. The building is highly influenced by the Bergen styles of the time. This building was the beginning of what eventually became Kvikne's Hotel in Balestrand. Behind the warehouse is a glimpse of the general store, and on the right is the first guesthouse building which had room for three or four visitors.
Photograph: Kvikne's Hotel, about 1870.

Another important source of inspiration for the development of these wooden buildings was the old half-timber construction as found in Germany and in much of France. During the 19th century, many buildings on the continent were still being built in half-timber. In Norway, wooden buildings usually were constructed of horizontal logs or planks and sided with wooden panels. Often, certain aspects of half-timber constructions were imitated with borders in the paneling to resemble joists and protruding beam ends. Ose Tourist Home has this kind of facade treatment.

In the north of France, parts of Germany and in the Alps, one can also find wooden roof constructions which both braced the overhanging roofs and provided exterior decoration. This was especially common in gables, where beam constructions at the outermost point under the protruding roof were shaped as diagonal crossed supports or a horizontal tie-beam joined with a suspended column which continued up to a ridge spire at the apex. These decorative gable designs beyond the vertical wall under the outermost part of the roof extension can be called floating gables, as they are in German. A floating gable design, which became very popular in Norway at the end of the 19th century, was an arched tie beam inserted in the gable triangle. Sources for this can be found in northern French half-timber houses, especially in Normandy. The arched beam construction gave the building a decorative aspect. Fleischer's Hotel and Hotel Union are both good examples of rich variations in floating gable constructions.

The ideal in this type of wooden architecture was that the construction should be visible. Many buildings give the impression that extra elements have been added to make them more decorative, and that these additions have no relationship with the construction. In addition, the constructions were decorated with thinner boards with cut-out ornaments, vine leaves and other plant forms which filled the space between the beams in an elegant manner. The facing gableboards and hanging bargeboards along the edges of the roof were sawed into tongues and scallops. Doors and windows received similar treatment. The widespread use of such decoration was an architectonic expression of the joy in

style of architecture. This period in architectural history (and for the applied arts as well) is called "historicism," because many so-called revival styles, such as Gothic and Renaissance Revival and Neo-Baroque, emerged, all based on historical architecture from the Middle Ages and from the 17th and 18th centuries. An important principle at that time was to use forms which were associated with the material used, and not just to render designs from stone architecture in wood. Old wooden building techniques and designs from different parts of Europe were sources of inspiration for newer wooden buildings. For that reason, it is equally correct to speak of historistic wooden architecture in different styles as it is to use the term "Swiss style." But, the use of the term "Swiss style" is widespread. It seems to have originated in connection with "Swiss roofs" as early as the middle of the 19th century. From there, it spread to all wooden houses from this period with roofs which project well beyond the outer walls. In this book, the term "Swiss style" is framed in quotation marks to emphasize that it does not necessarily refer to something particularly Swiss.

Switzerland and the other countries in the Alps, however, were a great source of inspiration, but that is seen primarily in the large projecting roofs, which were considered necessary to protect the wood from moisture damage. Other inspirations for large projecting roofs were 16th-century Italian country villas, so even this characteristic is not always of Swiss origin. And this is not made simpler when the roofs are steep. Roofs with pointed gables had been common in all of northern Europe during the Middle Ages and, in 19th-century architecture, are usually interpreted as characteristic of the Gothic Revival.

decoration with lace, fringes and frills in costume and in furniture, so typical of the times. In English, this type of wooden decoration is called gingerbread.

The decoration in wooden architecture also had historical sources in both the building tradition of the Alps and in the half-timbered architecture on the continent, where more time-consuming and costly wood-carving had been the norm. Another important source for this exterior decoration with beams and ornament was roof constructions found inside English churches and halls from the late Middle Ages. 19th-century architects happily adopted this kind of carved decor and simulated it in cheaper techniques involving contour-sawing, a technique which also suited more industrial mass-production, which gradually was developed by factories involved in the manufacture of woodwork. Indoors, this kind of decor was supplemented with painted ornament applied with stencils.

The new wooden architecture of the 19th century, as it was practiced in Norway, was primarily developed in Germany. At that time, there was no comprehensive training of architects in Norway, so architects usually completed their education at technical universities in Germany. This led to a close relationship between German and Norwegian architecture up to the time just before World War I.

Toward the end of the 19th century, Norway also developed its own variation of European wooden architecture. This was the so-called dragon style, usually with unpaneled log walls. The roofs often featured characteristic roof ridges, which ended in open-mouthed dragon heads over the gable apexes. This decoration was inspired by Norwegian stave churches from the Middle Ages, while the buildings themselves derived from old Norwegian store-houses and farmhouses with galleries or covered balconies. These designs became very popular in tourist architecture such as hotels and wanderers' cottages. The most prominent representatives were the different hotel and restaurant buildings at Holmenkollen and Frognerseteren (in the hills of Oslo). Other examples include Hotel Dalen, Tuddal Mountain Hotel and Sandven Hotel, where dragon style decor is combined with other European historical forms.

The veranda

The most prominent facade element in 19th-century wooden architecture was generally one or more verandas. These are distinguished from balconies and porches in that they are covered with a roof. Often they were built up in fantastic beam constructions, lavishly decorated with jigsaw decoration. The veranda was a new element which originated in the middle of the 19th century. It came to Norway from Germany, but it had originated in English architecture around 1800, in which verandas were constructed in stone, cast iron and wood around 1800. The veranda probably originated in India and other warm countries, where the roof provided shade against the oppressive heat. In "Swiss style" architecture, it is so common that it can be considered a trademark.

The veranda was a new concept of space, which was both outdoors and indoors at the same time. One could sit there in the open air and enjoy nature, while at the same time be protected against wind, rain and sun. Such additions became popular in private homes as well as in hotels and sanitariums. In wooden buildings, the verandas were built of beams in many of the same configurations known from earlier half-timber architecture. These construction plans were sometimes supplemented with the same designs used in floating gable constructions with arches and crossbeams. The space between the beams gave ample opportunity for decorating with jigsaw work in a wealth of patterns. The most successful example of this veranda-architecture in Norway was Kvikne's Hotel at Balestrand on the Sognefjord. Other exquisite examples can be found at Husum Hotel, Sandven and Hotel Dalen. After World War I, people indulged in more active outdoor activity, and the sun was no longer regarded as harmful, so

Guests at the sanitarium at Modum Spa in 1872. There were plenty of verandas to provide the guests with fresh air, but shaded enough to protect them from the sun and rain. The attire seems quite middle class, but compared to what was usual back then, the guests seem to be dressed for everyday living. Photograph: Drammen's Museum.

In the tourist hotels from the end of the 1800's, the dining rooms were often highly decorative. The most fantastic of all was the large Hotel Hardanger in Odda, which opened in 1896. It was bedecked with Lars Kinsarvik's dragon style carvings and Nils Bergslien's large paintings. At this time, it was usual to dine at refectory tables in the dining room, and here, guests were served by personnel suitably dressed in Hardanger regional costumes. After Odda became an industrial town, the hotel became the town hall in 1918. It was demolished in the 1970's. Photograph: Hardanger Open Air Museum, about 1900.

verandas decreased in popularity. In many places, they were enclosed, and in newer buildings, simpler balconies took their place.

Sanitariums

Architecturally, a sanitarium differed little from a tourist hotel. It was, nonetheless, a model which was used more frequently for treatment centers where patients stayed for a relatively long time. Common rooms, such as dining rooms and lounges, and perhaps a small number of guest bedrooms, often were concentrated in a central building, while most guests were lodged in smaller villas on the surrounding grounds. In the villas, there was enough room for larger families with servants, and it was even possible to keep one's own house, if desired.

An early example of this arrangement could be found at Modum Spa. It was developed by Dr. Thaulow in the 1850's, by a spring, called St. Olav's Source, which was said to have healing powers. The spa at Larvik was originally called "Sulfur Springs and Iodine Sulfur Spa," but after it was renamed for King Haakon VII, business improved. Now it is known as the source of Farris, Norway's popular sparkling mineral water. Another well-known resort in the hotel-villa style was Hankø Bath near Fredrikstad, where the regimen of the day was sea water and sea air combined with the scent of evergreens. Fresh air was important in the treatment of tuberculosis, and the architectural result of this can be seen in verandas and terraces. Lisbetsæter was originally this kind of treatment facility.

Neo-Baroque, Classical Revival and regionalism at the turn of the century

The "Swiss style" went out of fashion with architects around the turn of the century, but many local building contractors continued to build in that style into the 1920's. The new styles of architecture after World War I were inspired by sources from the 18th and early 19th centuries and are called Nordic Neo-Baroque and Classical Revival, depending upon the forms used. The buildings once again were given a more enclosed appearance, with a regular, simple rectangular floor plan. Roof projections became small and the roofs high and unifying, without the many gables and dormers which projected in many directions at the end of the 19th century. Facade decoration hearkened back to Greek and Roman classic shapes with columns and pilasters. Pilasters are flat, columnar forms on wall surfaces which mark the corners of a building and are used to break up long facades or to frame entrance portals. Ceilings were not so high as those of the previous century. Typical forms from this time can be seen at Haakonsæt Hotel and in the guest wing from 1924 at Sandven Hotel.

These shapes often could be drawn from old northern European sources. In wooden architecture, it was just as common to find models in our own building heritage in larger official residences and in the cities. During this time, shapes which had been popular in the appropriate parts of the country from the 1600's to the early 1800's were still in use. This resumption of regional building traditions provides the foundation for the definition of regionalist architecture. This architecture was often an unspoken reaction against the "Swiss style" and later modernism, which many considered foreign and undesirable. Rafoss Hotel in Kvinesdal is an example of this kind of southern Norwegian regionalism, while Walaker Hotel along the Sognefjord, built at around the same time, has western Norwegian characteristics.

Modernism, modernization and nostalgia

In the 1930's, new international ideals emerged once more with the clean lines and shapes of functionalism. This meant that a building's purpose and requirements should determine its shape and appearance, without the use of historical sources for style and decoration. Concrete walls and flat roofs were distinguishing features. Windows were often placed in a band over the facade, as in the 1937 glass veranda at Hotel Union. These ideals were developed further after World War II and are called late functionalism or modernism. Effectiveness and rationalism were important elements in planning, and shapes were freed from the decoration of earlier times.

Architecture was supposed to express new and modern times. The richly decorated architecture of the 19th century was looked down upon as both old-fashioned and ugly, and architects regarded it with disdain. They turned to monotonous surfaces with windows of one or two large single sheets of glass. Many hotels acquired new additions which did not suit the older buildings in any way. All hotel rooms were supposed to be the same, in order to satisfy the busloads of tourists who all had paid the same price and expected the same service. Fleischer's Hotel had such an addition for 35 years, and Kvikne's Hotel still has the biggest one of all. The banquet hall at Sandven Hotel also dates from this period.

Unrestrained modernism lasted almost until 1980, when a growing number of travelers and architects once again opened their eyes to the great charm and potential for well-being of the old hotels. Architectural adaptation has become a key phrase for many, and this principle has become more and more important in the planning of new additions at the old hotels. At the same time, many of the worst examples of modernistic and unsuitable additions have been altered to harmonize better with the original architecture. Fleischer's Hotel at Voss is an excellent example of this.

A common aspect in this century's modernization is a comprehensive rise in standards, especially in improved sanitary con-

ditions and modernization of the kitchens. Another kind of modernization includes fire prevention measures. Tragic hotel fires have led to more stringent rules, and this has led to the sectioning of buildings, the use of fire-retardant materials and safer escape routes. In addition, fire and smoke alarms have been installed and many hotels have sprinker systems.

These demands for comfort and security have brought about installations and alterations which have not necessarily contributed to any esthetic advantage. In some places, problems have been solved with carefully designed plans which have been made to conform to the original arrangements to a great degree. In other places, the commitment to retain the original surroundings is so strong that sometimes capacity has been reduced to avoid making disfiguring changes.

In many places, buildings and interiors have been modernized according to changing styles and tastes. In more recent times there has been an increasing tendency to return to the styles and shapes of earlier periods - although not necessarily back to the original in all details. This concerns nostalgia, a word which can have both positive and negative connotations, depending upon the views of those using it. Historical authenticity and quality of craftsmanship are important factors in evaluating the restoration of styles from an earlier time.

The hotels and guesthouses in this book represent quite a varied selection of the different building types and periods which are discussed here. Common to most of the buildings is that they have preserved much of their original appearance. The atmosphere of a time long gone is kept alive and serves as the foundation for an experience of both historical and cultural value.

The dragon style was very popular at many tourist complexes in the 1880's and 1890's. Many large buildings were erected at Holmenkollen and Frognerseteren, just outside the capital, as part of an attempt to attract people to the countryside for walks. The most expensive of them all was Holmenkollen Tourist Hotel, built in 1896, which is covered in intricate carvings and extensive artistic decoration. It was designed by architect Ole Sverre. This building replaced the original hotel on the site, which was destroyed by fire after only six years in operation. But in 1914, this building also fell prey to the flames. In the background on the left is the first sanitarium, Midstuen, from 1891, which still stands by the road leading up to what is now Holmenkollen Park Hotel Rica. Photograph: Skøien, about 1900, National Office of Historic Monuments archives.

HOLMENKOLLEN PARK HOTEL RICA
Oslo

A fairy tale castle overlooking the city

"Tree-covered hills and grassy mountainsides with rivers and ponds and peaceful farms...miles inward toward the north, east and west. In the south, open to Oslofjord...a dazzling view of Norway's beautiful capital, surrounded by islands, rocks, sounds and sea.

That describes Holmenkollen, the hill with the famous name. And it's the setting for Holmenkollen Tourist Hotel & Sanitarium, on the slope facing south, with the forest behind and the magnificent panorama in front, and it welcomes you to a relaxing and refreshing stay.

The hotel buildings rise above dry bedrock, 350 meters above sea level, like a fairy tale castle. Grand driveways lead the way up to the hotel. Beautiful, sheltered trails are everywhere – far into the dense, peaceful forests – to Holmenkollen hill, where Europe's most famous ski race is held every March – to Frognerseteren, the well-known café where sporty young people meet on Sundays and in the evenings – to Tryvann Stadium with Europe's highest skating rink, where, on a winter day, you can see Olympic champions train, or maybe even Sonja Henie dancing across the shining surface – to the Royal Lodge, where you can wave to the two little princesses, who romp under the eyes of their parents, the Crown Prince and Princess, and their grandparents, King Haakon and Queen Maud.

From your window in the hotel, you can look down over the city at the foot of the mountain, at the breadth of the fjord; Oslo, with beautiful medieval Akershus castle near the proud city hall, Norway's largest and most beautiful building, erected by the city's own citizens. Oslo, the residence of King Haakon and Queen Maud. Home of Henrik Ibsen, Fridtjof Nansen, Roald Amundsen, Edvard Munch..."

With these words, Holmenkollen Tourist Hotel presents itself and its surroundings in a brochure from 1935.

The hotel has one of Oslo's finest views. From its balconies, one can see the city and its surroundings, with the fjord and forest-clad hillsides.

The grand staircase is richly decorated in the dragon style expressed in carving, painting and textiles (right).

The fantastic architectural shapes found at Holmenkollen Park Hotel Rica were inspired by old Norwegian stave churches, cottages, and traditional mountain storehouses (previous pages).

The hotel's gourmet restaurant, "De Fem Stuer" (The Five Rooms), is in the old building which originally housed the dining room and lounges (left).

A fireside table in one of the dining rooms.

Much has changed since then! The capital has grown and buildings climb higher and higher up the side of Holmenkollen hill. The two small princesses, Astrid and Ragnhild, have been adults for many years, and their parents and grandparents are gone. But the beautiful old hotel at Holmenkollen is still there, overlooking the city, with one of the best views in town. For more than 100 years, it has been one of Oslo's greatest tourist attractions – a proud monument to the unique Norwegian dragon style. Today, it's part of exclusive Holmenkollen Park Hotel Rica, with guests from around the world.

Lung specialist and founder

It was not always that way. When the building was new, it was called Holmenkollen Sanitarium, and patients, not hotel guests, found their way to the wooden castle at Holmenkollen. But, let's not get ahead of things...

Dr. Ingebrigt Christian Lund Holm, born in Skien in 1844, built both sanitarium and hotel. He wanted to give as many people as possible the most important conditions for general well-being and good health, and this meant light, air, water and outdoor living. After becoming a doctor in Christiania in 1872, he opened a practice in Larvik, where he discovered a sulfuric spring near the Farris River, later called "King Haakon's Source," and he established Larvik Spa in 1880. In 1878, however, Dr. Holm moved to Christiania, where he specialized in pulmonary diseases. He established an inhalation institution and practiced as a lung specialist, while at the same time, he ran Larvik Spa. In 1883, he took the initiative for Christiania Baths, on the site where Torvgata Baths later was built. He was administrative director and medical leader here until 1895, and it was here he introduced the "sauna bath." At the same time, he was often a consultant for new baths and spas throughout the country.

Dr. Holm's next great project was to open Holmenkollen and Voksenkollen to the people of Christiania. Since the 1870's, he had dreamed of building a sanitarium here, and after he purchased a 100-acre tract from the Holmenkol-Voxenkol Company for NOK 10,000, he could finally realize his dream. He established a corporation with brewery owner Ellef Ringnes and wholesaler Alfred Larsen and called it Holmenkollen Tourist Hotel & Sanitarium.

The adventure begins

Dr. Holm hired architect Holm Munthe, who also had designed Larvik Spa, to plan both the hotel, the sanitarium and the restaurants. The tourist hotel was the first project, planned and built in two stages, and finished around Easter, 1890. The hotel quickly became a popular destination for the people of Oslo, and the better part of the hotel was turned into cafés and restaurants. In the end, there was room for only 15 guests. That was not Dr. Holm's intention, so he immediately began work on a sanitarium alongside the hotel. It opened in the summer of 1891 and was geared for people who suffered from different ailments, but not tuberculosis and other contagious diseases. Here they could enjoy light, air, water and the great outdoors. And they come in droves! When Holmenkollbakken ski jump was constructed and the yearly national ski race was moved here from Huseby hill, the new sanitarium soon became too small. Dr. Holm then built a new and larger sanitarium, which opened in 1894.

On March 31 the following year, there was a catastrophe. The popular tourist hotel, which had opened only five years earlier,

The dining rooms are good examples of the Norwegian national romantic style of the 1890's, complete with log walls and art of the period, such as Gerhard Munthe's painting from Hallingdal.

Dr. Holm had resigned from the management of the hotel and sanitarium at Holmenkollen in 1905, in order to begin a new project, Dr. Holm's Hotel at Geilo. There were many plans for rebuilding the hotel at Holmenkollen, but they were never realized. Instead, the sanitarium, which had opened in 1894, and which had the same management as the tourist hotel, was converted into a hotel.

From hotel to course center

The years passed. The hotel was a popular destination, both for weekend stays and vacations, and the people of Oslo visited it frequently. After the Second World War broke out, the Germans seized the hotel and turned it into a residence for the occupiers. During that period, the beautiful building was ravaged, and log walls and carvings were painted over. After the war, the Norwegian Military Command took over the hotel and used it as a temporary residence for Norwegian officers and their families who had returned from England and the United States.

During the summer of 1947, the hotel was released and then sold to a corporation consisting of lawyer Harald Ram and restaurateurs, Hans Telle and Jacob Berg. Immediately, they began a thorough restoration and modernization, and the venerable hotel was reopened in May, 1948. In the following years, the hotel was considered one of Oslo's most exclusive, favored by royal guests from around the world. It was the natural center of attraction during the yearly Holmenkollen races, and the Royal Lunch at Holmenkollen Tourist Hotel became a regular yearly tradition.

Through the years, plans for extensions were launched but never realized. When Ramm died in 1970, the hotel was sold to NEMI, North European Management Institute, an institution established for further education of executives. For the next seven years, it was used primarily as a course center for NEMI, until the organization was disbanded. One of the owners, shipowner Leif Høegh, bought out the others and took over the hotel on January 1, 1978.

A hotel once more

Now, plans for extending the hotel were begun. Just before the 1982 World Championships in skiing began in Oslo, the new hotel opened its doors under the name of Holmenkollen Park

burned to the ground. The cause of the fire is still uncertain, but a candle may have fallen on the floor and ignited an old woven rug.

From sanitarium to hotel

It didn't take long before construction was begun on a new hotel, this one designed by architect Ole Sverre, Holm Munthe's assistant. It was a beautiful building, twice the size of the old hotel. With its numerous verandas, carved dragonheads on the gables and intricate wood carving in many other places, it looked like a fantastic castle straight out of a Norwegian fairy tale. Assisted by its unique setting, it became one of the most popular sights in Oslo almost from its opening day in 1896. In 1898, Holmenkollbanen (metro) opened, and at the end station – the present Besserud station – passengers boarded covered carriages which brought them to the hotel. Now it was both simpler and easier to get there, so even more visitors made their way to the hotel.

But as with its predecessor and many other dragon style buildings, it, too, burned down. During the night of July 10, 1914, it was struck by lightning, and in only two hours, the beautiful building was reduced to a pile of ashes.

Hotel. A new addition with 150 guest bedrooms was built, and the capital acquired a modern and much-needed hotel. It is still owned by the Høegh family, but in 1986, they turned over the management to Rica, Norway's largest privately-owned hotel chain, therefore the name, Holmenkollen Park Hotel Rica.

Today, the old sanitarium at Holmenkollen is part of a large, modern hotel. The beautiful old building has been meticulously restored and houses the hotel's restaurant, banquet and conference rooms. And the wooden building on one of Oslo's best lots with a view is still a big tourist attraction.

The old main building of Holmenkollen Park Hotel, or Holmenkollen Sanitarium, which it was called when it opened in 1894, sits like a fairy tale castle on a hill overlooking Oslo. With its extreme dragon style shapes inspired by old Norwegian wooden houses and stave churches, it is an excellent example of the national romantic style. The part about the fairy tale can be taken literally, for one of the creators of the dragon style has stated that he was inspired by fairy tale illustrations when he designed the original Holmenkollen Hotel in similar shapes some years earlier.

Even the colors on the outer facade are close to the original. In an enthusiastic article about the new building in 1894, the architects' trade journal wrote that the hotel was stained reddish-brown, which clearly was uncommon. Nor was the blue-green color used for decoration, but the magazine felt that it "well suits the somber spruce trees, which closely surround the building,

"A modern, though not a wide road" was built up to the complex. The long wide corridors were well suited for promenades in bad weather. Electric lights, very advanced conveniences for the time, were powered by the building's own gasoline-powered generator.

Inside, the building is very well preserved, with its walls of planed round logs and painted decor. The massive doors are important links, along with the patterned beamed ceilings, and the powerful wainscoting in the dining room is in keeping with the style of the time. In conjunction with the expansion of the hotel and the extensive restoration of the main building in 1982, some older rooms were converted into lounges and meeting rooms for the hotel's conference division. Large paintings by famous artists from the time the hotel was built are an important part of the interior.

In 1982, a new guest wing was built behind the hotel, where there had been an annex at the turn of the century. The new wing was constructed in the modern idiom, and the new rooms were organized in blocks along the crest of the hill. Now, one can really speak of long promenade corridors. The architect was Stein Aasen. Later, there have been several smaller extensions with new buildings in the area, and the guest wing has been extended even more.

A fairy tale castle

The present hotel was designed by architect Balthazar Lange (1854-1937), who won the assignment in a competition. Ten years earlier, he had designed some hunting lodges, which helped to create the typical Norwegian log cabin, which is now a part of Norwegian vacation home architecture.. The hotel is one of the largest buildings in the country constructed of unpaneled logs, and the large body of the building is organized into two large wings at angles to one another. The building components are harmoniously grouped in smaller blocks connected both crosswise and lengthwise, and with each successive floor projecting slightly over the previous one. A large tower inspired by the stave churches at Borgund in Lærdal and Heddal in Telemark, crowns the intersection of the wings. Less frightening leafy formations which curl up over the ends of the gables have been used instead of the dragon heads typical of stave churches. Many large verandas contribute to variation in the facades. These are constructed with details from stave churches and from the galleries of old Norwegian log houses. The large roof projections have been borrowed from European wooden architecture of the period. This is a Norwegian version of that era's international hotel architecture.

Originally, the main entrance was in the corner on the courtyard side, and the original entrance portal, with its wealth of carving, leads into the ornate stairwell. The columns and guardrails are inspired by shapes in many stave churches and feature carvings decorated with stencils in reddish-brown and green on oiled wood.

The old main building at Holmenkollen Park Hotel still stands much as it did when it was first built as a sanitarium in 1894. Early 20th-century photograph, National Office of Historic Monuments archives.

The hotel at Holmenkollen was part of a larger group of buildings in the dragon style, in which the dragons, with their gaping jaws and carved and painted decoration, stretched beyond the apexes of the gables. During the 1890's, the area around Holmenkollen had many dragon style buildings, including restaurants, cafés, hotels and a chapel. This was the architectonic expression of something completely new in Norwegian culture at that time — that great numbers of people set out on long walks in the forests and fields on their free days, both summer and winter. This is not at all common in other countries, and the dragon style buildings at Holmenkollen and Frognerseteren stand as monuments to the development of this specifically Norwegian phenomenon.

SYGARD GRYTTING

Harpefoss

It started with pilgrims...

The traditional estate of Sygard Grytting lies along European Route 6, between Hundorp and Vinstra, 70 kilometers north of Lillehammer. High up and unobstructed, with a fantastic view over the green-clad slopes and snow-topped mountains of Sør Fron, it dominates the landscape from its sunny, southern slope. Here the valley is open and wide, making this is one of the best agricultural districts in Gudbrandsdal valley. There has been farming at Sygard Grytting since time immemorial, and both the farm and the surrounding area are rich in archaeological remains from pagan times. Archaeologists believe that Sygard Grytting was the valley's power base until around 600 AD, when it was moved five kilometers south to Dale Gudbrand's farm at Hundorp.

Today, the big old farm complex at Sygard Grytting is one of the best preserved in Gudbrandsdal and is a unique historical example of the distinctive building style in this area. Most of the 25 buildings on the farm are notched log constructions, scorched brown by the weather, wind, and sands of time. 14 of these buildings create a double courtyard, consisting of an inner and an outer yard.

Hundreds of years of family idyll

There are four original dwelling houses in the inner courtyard at Sygard Grytting with a combined living space of 850 square meters. At the top of the courtyard is Øvre (Upper), the home of the hosts, Hilde Nustad Grytting and Stig Skurdal Grytting. Sygard Grytting had been run by the same family since 1534, and Hilde and Stig are the 18th owners of the farm since then. The farm has, in all likelihood, been in the same ownership since 1300, but this is, as yet, undocumented.

The oldest building in the inner courtyard is Gamleloftet (the old loft), a renovated medieval sleeping loft. This heritage building is believed to date from around 1300. It can also be characterized as Gudbrandsdal's oldest surviving "tourist complex," as a letter on parchment from 1343 mentions "Svævnstova," now Gamleloftet at Sygard Grytting. Then, as now, the main road between Oslo and Trondheim went through Gudbrandsdal, and

Gamleloftet served as an inn for travelers, including pilgrims on their way to St. Olaf's grave at Nidaros (Trondheim). It is known that King Magnus Magnusson spent the night here in 1311.

Otherwise, the inner courtyard consists of the old main building, Inne (Inside) from the end of the 1600's, and Nedre (Lower) from the middle of the 1800's. These buildings comprise today's hotel.

Nedre becomes a boarding house

Stig's great-great-grandfather, Ola P. Grytting, built fancy Nedre house. It was most likely built to increase his standing, for having many houses on a farm was a sign of prosperity in previous times. There is little to show that he needed more space, because when the house was finished, it was rented out to the first country doctor in Fron and Ringebu. The house was later used as a school. After that, it functioned as an administration building for the railroad, during the expansion of the railroad line from Tretten to Otta. When the new line was opened in 1896 and the railroad people left the area, it became a school for wood carvers.

In 1917, Anna Grytting, the sister of Stig's grandfather, opened Grytting Farm and Boarding House. Anna was born and raised on the farm, but as a young girl, she had moved to Kristiania and gone into service with a clergyman and his family. She was unhappy in the capital and spent her time thinking that there must be a way to use all the buildings on the farm for something profitable. She moved back to her home area and made Nedre into a boarding house. The Russian Revolution had just ended, and the

In the Nedre guest building, meals are served in the kitchen.
Old Gudbrandsdal traditions are kept alive here.

Sygard Grytting lies high and free in the wide Sør-Fron countryside.
On the right, with the white gable, is Nedre guesthouse with most of the guest bedrooms (next pages).

Restoration and the Olympics

The current hosts at Sygard Grytting took over the venerable farm in 1989. They left Oslo, where Hilde studied ergotherapy and Stig worked as an engineer, to become farmers in their home district. With 50 acres of cultivated land, sheep, grain cultivation, and forestry, there was plenty to do. Stig and Hilde wanted to restore the old buildings on the farm, but they did not know where they would get the money for the project.

The solution was the Lillehammer Olympics and Queen Sonja's proposal to use large farms around Lillehammer to house royalty and other prominent guests during the games. No royals came to Sygard Grytting, but the Queen's initiative still produced results. During the time before the Olympics, the LOOC (Lillehammer Olympic Organizing Committee) used Sygard Grytting, among others, for entertaining visitors. In addition, the main sponsors for the Norwegian alpine skiing team rented the estate for use by their administration during the games.

Hilde and Stig are the current hosts at Sygard Grytting. They stand in front of the Øvre building with its beautiful Neo-Classical portals.

This room in Nedre guesthouse is covered with reproductions of the room's oldest wallpaper, dating from around the middle of the 1800's. Otherwise, one of the house's many Neo-Classical doors and Biedermeier furniture are visible here.

A detailing from the dining room in Nedre guesthouse where the glazed blue wall paintings have been carefully restored (left).

first guests at the boarding house at Sygard Grytting were 17 Russian officers who had escaped from the revolution in their homeland. They stayed almost a year. Eventually, Anna's sister, Gunda, returned home. She had attended business school, home economics school and a gourmet cooking school, and she left her job as manager at Rjukan Tourist Hotel to help her sister run the boarding house. They advertised clean, fresh air; well-prepared and hearty food; and fresh eggs, milk, and cream produced on the farm. Soon the place became a popular recreation and holiday spot for city dwellers who wanted to relax and gather strength in beautiful and healthy surroundings.

With this, Hilde and Stig had secured an economic base for their restoration of the old buildings. Now time was of the essence, and by the time the Lillehammer games opened in February 1994, most of the houses on the farm were refurbished. The renovation and restoration was so carefully done, that one year later, Hilde and Stig were awarded the Historical Preservation Society's Protection Award for Oppland, for the outstanding manner in which they had preserved the old, authentic milieu on the farm.

From Olympic farm to hotel

The restored farm was teeming with life during the Olympics, and the guests were more than pleased with their stay. After the Olympics were over, Hilde and Stig decided to revive the old boarding house traditions from Anna and Gunda's time.

Today Sygard Grytting is one of Norway's most beautiful and distinctive small hotels. The Nedre and Inne buildings form a regular hotel, while in the old "men's hut," where the farmhands used to live, there are self-catering rooms.

A stay at Sygard Grytting is a stay in real rural surroundings, with beautiful and impressive countryside all around. It is an ideal starting point for mountain walks, and for fishing in the many mountain lakes, or in Gudbrandsdal, at the very bottom of the valley. It is only a short trip to many attractions, such Dale-Gudbrand's farm, where the pagan chieftain Dale-Gudbrand met Olav Haraldson in 1021, and Sør Fron church, also known as "Gudbrandsdal Cathedral," a beautiful octagonal stone church from 1787.

But – the most beautiful attraction is still Sygard Grytting farm, where the boarding house tradition has developed over many hundreds of years, from a pilgrim inn to today's comfortable, yet carefully preserved, guesthouse. In connection with Trondheim's jubilee in 1997, the old pilgrim route will again be marked. To coincide with this, the restoration of Gamleloftet at Sygard Grytting will be finished. Perhaps, there will be a few pilgrims as well as tourists at the farm.

The atmospheric guest room in the old main building, Inne.
Modern comforts have been tastefully and carefully integrated into the
old milieu.

The well-preserved old group of farm buildings at Sygard Grytting has crowned the same place on the side of the valley since around 1780, when many older houses were moved from the old road up to the Royal Road, which was constructed at the beginning of the 18th century. The road was rerouted again around 1860, and European Route 6 now is a safe distance below.

The grouping of the buildings is typical for the region of Gudbrandsdal, with its division into two rectangular courtyards – the outer courtyard, with buildings

those usually found in structures dating from the Middle Ages in other valleys, but they are similar to those in other medieval buildings in this valley.

The present main building, Øvre, the residence of the host and hostess, is composed of two older houses. One is from around 1720, while the other probably dates from the end of the 1700's. When they were joined, a central hall was constructed straight through the house from the main entrance. This entry portal has a two-sashed door with faceted door panels and is framed by windows with intricate

and other fixtures. The lounge features three sitting groups in Classical Revival and Biedermeier styles, typical for large farms in eastern Norway during the middle of the 19th century. One group has been on the farm for generations, as have most of the other furnishings in the house. The chandelier was installed when the farm got electricity.

The former main building, Inne, is probably from the end of the 18th century, but it contains parts of a much older building. Its classic three-room layout, with one large and two small rooms, was the norm

Solid farm traditions

for animals and feed, and the inner courtyard with dwellings along with a storehouse and loft for food and clothing. The buildings are representative of larger farms in mid-Gudbrandsdal during the 18th and at the beginning of the 19th centuries. Apart from a few newer paneled additions and smaller sheds, all the buildings have their old log walls. Most roofs are covered with slate, as was typical for old buildings in the valley.

The newest outhouse is the long cowshed dating from the early 1870's. It is parallel with the large log barn which is from approximately 1800. The stable, with its impressive two-story gallery, dates from around 1780. The outer courtyard also includes a small pigsty.

The inner courtyard is a harmonious rectangular area surrounded by two-story log buildings on all four sides. The present main building, Øvre (Upper), and the storehouse are on the upper long side, while the guest building, Nedre (Lower), is on the lower side. The former main building, Inne (Inside), is at one short end, and across, in the far end of the inner courtyard, is the legendary sleeping loft from the Middle Ages.

This loft building was described at the end of the 18th century as a very large building from Catholic times, which previously was supposed to have had three floors. There were traces left from many beds, and it once had arched entry doors decorated with carvings. In 1785, it was said that the building had been torn down a few years earlier. Present researchers have problems interpreting the old accounts, but they have established that the loft building which now stands there is made of ancient logs, in which the notches are carved in a special way which has not been used since the Black Death of 1350. The length of the logs indicates that the building is still the original size, but the third floor remains a mystery. It is presumed that the loft as it stands today is largely composed of logs from the old sleeping loft dating from around 1780, when the courtyard was moved. The logs in the building have smaller dimensions than

Sygard Grytting has remained almost unchanged for a long time. It looked like this when it was a boarding house around 1930.
"Well-prepared hearty food; clean and with good service" states an ad from that time.
Photograph: Property of the farm.

crosspieces. Richly carved garlands decorate the tops of the portal windows. According to tradition on the farm, the doors date from around 1860, but the entire arrangement is typical of the Neo-Classicism of the first half of the 19th century.

The guest building, Nedre, also has a center portal, but of a simpler shape. It was probably built around 1860, and the doors and moldings throughout also are typical of the Classical Revival in its rural form. Inside, there is a large sitting room, a middle room, dining room and kitchen in the first floor, while there are five guest rooms on the second floor. The entire building is restored with great sensitivity for the original arrangement, and old fixtures have been preserved where possible. The sitting room has wainscoting and old wallpaper. Custom-made reproductions of the oldest wallpapers from the room below and the guest rooms above have been used. When showers and toilets were added to the guest rooms, materials and details which were already in the house were used, in order to retain the feeling of the original building. This is also true for modernization of the kitchen, where old cupboards were models for new. All rooms are equipped with antique furniture

in the countryside all over southern Norway. The staircase in this two-story building is outside in the gallery. The upper larger room or hall on the second floor is used as a conference and dining room for larger groups. The planed panel walls are typical for large farms in eastern Norway around 1800. There is also a guestroom with log walls and old furniture on this floor.

The men's cottage is more rustic. It has been at the edge of the courtyard since around 1870, but the building itself is somewhat older. The entry doors may date from the beginning of the 18th century. There is a new kitchen area in the living room with the large fireplace, which also features a long, traditional table and other old furniture. Among other pieces are Renaissance style chairs which usually date to the 1600's. The loft was recently raised with old logs to make room for four box beds attached to the walls. The floor and newer furnishings are of massive, hand-planed wood. Antique balcony furniture can be found outside in the gallery, which here serves as a balcony. Few farms in Gudbrandsdal have so many old buildings still standing and are so well-maintained and restored as this one.

KONGSVOLD MOUNTAIN LODGE
Dovre

In the heart of Dovrefjell National Park

Kongsvold Mountain Lodge lies along European Route 6, right in the middle between Dombås and Oppdal. The wonderful location, at the top of Drivdal valley, 900 meters above sea level, in the heart of Dovrefjell (mountain) National Park, makes it a popular destination for hikers, explorers and nature lovers alike. Knutshøen, Europe's most famous green mountain, looms behind the hotel. For over 200 years, the mountains at Dovre have been renowned for their rich flora. 420 plant species are registered at Dovrefjell National Park and Protected Area. A short walk from Kongsvold Mountain Lodge to Knutshøen leads to a number of these species. The rich, luxuriant, and varied vegetation at Dovre hosts abundant bird life. During the summer months, gray thrush, willow grouse, bluethroats, meadow pipits, golden plovers, Lapland longspurs, and many others can be studied at close range.

The mountains northwest of Kongsvold are home to Norway's musk oxen. These rare, peaceful herbivores were first introduced in the 1930's, but they disappeared during the war. From 1947 to 1953, 23 calves from eastern Greenland were introduced. Since then, the flock of musk oxen has grown to around 50 animals. Kongsvold Mountain Lodge is a central starting point for foot tours into the habitat of the musk ox and the large herd of wild reindeer at Dovre, as well as an excellent place for hunting or fishing. Mammals and birds are protected year-round, but the hunting of wild reindeer, ptarmigan, hare, red fox, and mink is permitted in accordance with applicable rules. Kongsvold Mountain Lodge offers the sports fisherman rivers and mountain lakes teeming with trout.

From a self-service cabin to a mountain lodge

From time immemorial, the road across Dovrefjell has linked eastern Norway with Trøndelag. Access to Nidaros (Trondheim), the royal seat, was the most important reason to cross the mountains. This traffic increased after Olav Haraldsson was canonized, making Nidaros one of Europe's most visited pilgrim sites.

For hundreds of years, the only way to cross the mountains was either by foot or on horseback. Travel by horse and carriage is first mentioned in 1704, but it was not commonplace until the end of the 18th century.

A journey over the mountains was both strenuous and more than a little dangerous. The Sagas tell us that King Øystein (1103-1123) had a way-station built at Dovre. This was the Viking equivalent of today's self-service cabin, and it was meant to make the journey over the mountains safer for travelers. Later, these cabins were manned, and from then on, they were called mountain lodges. Men were hired to keep the cabins clean and to guide people over the mountains during the winter. These men were tenants of the state, and their numerous duties and privileges were the backbone of the mountain hostel system. In the beginning, their duties were to feed and shelter travelers crossing the mountains, and to guide them onward. In 1734, these men were given the additional duties of providing postal service and transportation for hire to travelers. Their privileges consisted mainly of a grain tax, which the mountain hostels, with the king's approval, could demand from the local grain farmers in specified nearby settlements. In addition, there were tax exemptions and hunting, fishing, and pasture privileges. Dovrefjell had four such mountain lodges – Drivstua, Hjerkinn, Fokstua, and Kongsvold.

From Hullet to Kongsvold

Kongsvold Mountain Lodge is the youngest of those mentioned above, and today consists of 20 well-kept old buildings. The red and white painted houses blend well with the

The tavern has an extensive display of old tools and antiques which have followed the mountain lodge through the ages. There is also an informational display about Dovre mountains' flora and fauna (right).

The area surrounding Kongsvold Mountain Lodge is known for its rich flora, and the botanical mountain garden just south of the lodge is a prime attraction. It also serves as the headquarters for Kongsvold biological station. In addition, there is a weather station run by the Meteorological Institute.

Despite its location high up in the mountains, Kongsvold Mountain Lodge is reminiscent of an old estate (left).

surrounding landscape. Today, Kongsvold Mountain Lodge is owned by the Norwegian Department of the Environment and has been carefully restored in cooperation with the National Office of Historic Monuments.

Originally, the settlement was called Hullet (the Hollow) and lay two kilometers further down the valley. Hullet officially became a mountain hostel in 1670, and in 1704, King Frederik IV decided that it should be called Kongsvold. During the Great Nordic War of 1718, the Swedes, under the leadership of general Armfeldt, captured much of Trøndelag, and the Northern Mountain Dragoon regiment fled south across the mountains. The Norwegian forces burned down all four Dovre hostels at Dovre, including Kongsvold. In 1720, Kongsvold was rebuilt at its present site, and the first floor of the main building presumably dates from this time. Nedre (Lower) building and one of the storehouses date from the 1700's.

Once a survival station

The Kongsvold family have supervised the running of the lodge for over 300 years, since Jon Eriksen was hired to man the hostel in 1670. They have managed to keep in step with developments, and made sure that the lodge has kept up with the times to become today's comfortable mountain lodge.

In the beginning, the hostel was a survival station for travelers and functioned much like the simple inns of old. But the earlier

mentioned grain tax was just as important as the income from refreshments and guest rooms. This was the basis for the prosperity at Kongsvold during the 1800's. It lost an important part of its revenue when the grain tax was abolished in 1845 and replaced with an annual sum from the state treasury. With time, the roads and railroad were expanded, and the need for the lodge diminished. The hosts at Kongsvold mountain hostel had to change their focus to tourists. They were successful, and at the same time, they had income from both the rural post office and the local telephone exchange. Business continued to blossom.

The lodge had been state-owned, but in the years after the Dovre Railroad opened in 1921, the state saw their role as mountain innkeepers over. They sold the lodges to the families who had run them for generations. In 1935, the eighth generation of the Kongsvold family – Lina F. Kongsvold and Sigurd Holaker – bought the lodge. Lina left her mark on this period at Kongsvold. She continued to run the business in the old traditional way and was widely known for her hospitality.

Tradition lives on

Lina and Sigurd's son, Per Bjørn Holaker, who gradually took over the business from his parents, was a lawyer. His greatest interests, however, were in the fields of natural science, hunting, fishing, and outdoor life. He worked enthusiastically for the Dovrefjell region to be declared a national park, with the Kongsvold property included. He therefore willed the property to the Norwegian Department of the Environment. Unfortunately, he never saw his idea realized. He died in 1973, one year before the national park was created. Today, Mari Vigerust Rungul and her husband Bjørn Rangul run the Lodge. They were hired as hosts at Kongsvold in 1988. Mari is actually a relative of Per Bjørn Holaker. In this way,

The main lounge features both urban and rustic antiques from different eras.

Kongsvold's oldest cupboard is in the dining room. It was made during the 1600's and is decorated with Renaissance carving portraying the crucified Jesus flanked by Maria and Joseph.

The dining room. The numerous old and beautiful cupboards are characteristic of Kongsvold Mountain Lodge. The menu features traditional Norwegian food made with fresh local ingredients (right).

the old family traditions live on in these historical surroundings at Dovrefjell. Even though the state owns these lovely buildings filled with antique treasures collected over hundreds of years, Mari and Bjørn run it as if it were their own home. Hospitality and local food traditions are of prime importance at Kongsvold Mountain Lodge. Everything served is home-baked, homemade and inspired by local ingredients. The menu features musk ox sausage, reindeer tongue, smoked reindeer meat, dried and salted reindeer meat, elk burgers, and sour cream porridge. Just as it should be at a real lodge in the heart of Dovrefjell National Park.

Mari Vigerust Rangul serves guests at Kongsvold Mountain Lodge traditional Norwegian food prepared with local ingredients..

The buildings at Kongsvold, high up in the mountains, resemble a large Trøndelag farm. One can see that it was constructed to house travelers with their horses and carriages, but all the same, the local building tradition is evident in the houses.

The clutch of farm buildings is divided into an inner grouping with dwellings and storehouses and an outer one with stables and barns. The two groupings lie stretched out along the old Royal Road which forms a street between the many houses. In earlier days, roads were built like this, from farm to farm, until modern, motorized traffic became so annoying

building had a richly decorated two-story veranda on the courtyard side. It was built in the "Swiss style," and featured panes of colored glass on the side walls. With large openings at the front of the building, it was not particularly suited for the climate, when snowstorms raged over the high mountain region. Now the veranda is reduced to a small entryway on one floor.

The garden south of the main building's kitchen wing, built around 1890, is another more urban phenomenon. It was laid out with decorative small gravel paths in ornate circular patterns for promenades. In 1923, a new garden was planted farther

Fantstuggu, (the Tramps' House), which is very old and was built from logs from at least two older buildings. Originally, servant girls lived here, and around 1900, it was used for travelers who were not respectable enough to mix with others. Earlier, the present smithy was used for such people.

Guest bedroom standards have improved all along. After the state assumed ownership, the entire complex has undergone extensive repairs and improvements, primarily in the 1970's and 1980's. Bathrooms have been installed in many rooms, and some buildings have been remodeled for other purposes.

Rich folk art and building traditions in Trøndelag

that new roads were constructed away from the houses.

The special Trøndelag character at Kongsvold is visible in the long farmhouses, especially in the 18th-century building called Nedre (lower) at a right angle to the direction of the road between the main building and Kroa (the Inn). It is both long and very narrow, which was typical for Trøndelag farms for a long time. This style of house with a long facade is all over Trøndelag, but its first expression was in the long city "palaces" of Trondheim on their large lots. Stiftsgården, from the 1770's, is the most impressive building of this type. These long farmhouses are called Trønderlån – long Trønder buildings – and the design became so popular that when additions were needed, they were just added onto the ends, making the houses even longer. This custom is quite different from that of Gudbrandsdal on the other side of Dovrefjell (mountain,) where the houses traditionally have been much shorter and wider. Large portals with skylights and grand door frames were also incorporated into the elegant facades. Columns or somewhat simpler pilasters (flat columns attached to the wall) as in this case, often were used in the frames.

As late as the 1870's, all the houses at Kongsvold still showed their unpaneled notched logs, which probably stood in their natural, weather-beaten brown or gray. Toward the end of the last century, many of the houses were paneled and painted white, while the barns usually were painted red. The main building probably still includes parts of the first building from 1720, after all the mountain lodges at Dovre were burned down before the Swedes could advance that far during the Great Nordic War. It was a simple one-story dwelling with an extra floor which covered only part of the house, as was the norm in the Oppdal area in earlier days. This house was extended to two complete floors in the first half of the 19th century. The addition on the back, where the kitchen is now, was built in 1896. In an extension of the main building at the north end, the salon building was erected in 1888. As its name indicates, lounges were furnished for the guests, while there were new guest bedrooms in the floor above. Originally, the salon

Kongsvold Mountain Lodge around 1870. On the right is the main building from 1720, which, over the years, had been extended and enlarged to become two full floors in the Trøndelag style. On the left is Nedre guesthouse. At this time, none of the houses had wooden paneling. Photograph: Knud Knudsen, Kongsvold Mountain Lodge.

away from the building and features a large selection of the rich flora found in this mountainous region.

The largest storehouse to the north was built in 1781, and the smaller one alongside may be just as old. Nordre house, south of these, was moved from Sæteren in Drivdalen (valley) to Kongsvold in 1887 and has a small recessed gallery over the entrance. The barn, with its cowshed and bridge to the hayloft, was built in 1884 and is typical for farm buildings of the time. Above the barn is the large log building Raulåna, which originally was a stable with a hayloft above, when it was built around 1880. Its walls contain logs from many older buildings, as do other houses at Kongsvold. Both the earlier stable and the barn previously had two bridges to the upper floors. Raulåna was converted into the main building of a biological research station in 1979.

Farthest south in the complex is the so-called

Of the many other buildings, Kroa deserves to be mentioned in its own right. It consists of two old storehouses moved here from Folldal in 1884 and then connected with a wagon shed in paneled half-timber. This converted the two old log houses into one building. Inside, two log walls are visibly weather-beaten, since they were outer walls for many years before the move to Kongsvold. One part was used for pressing bed linens, while the other was the workers' kitchen. In 1960, it was converted to a roadside restaurant. The rich decoration, with antiques and rustic accessories found on site, was unusual at such places at the time and attracted a great deal of attention. In the cellar is an information center with exhibitions on botany, geology and ecology – and of course on the history of Kongsvold.

Kongsvold was well off in earlier days. That can be seen in more than just the impressive group of buildings. It is also visible in the extensive amount of furnishings which have been collected and displayed throughout, including excellent examples of rustic antiques, including tall clocks, cupboards and desks. Many feature typical carving with acanthus leaves from Gudbrandsdal. In furniture from the Trøndelag, curved door and cupboard panels and painted tendrils with leaves and flowers are a more important part of the decor.

BÅRDSHAUG MANOR
Orkanger

The government minister's old home

Beautiful Bårdshaug Manor, 40 kilometers from Trondheim, in the center of Orkanger, is surrounded by a large park, a miniature copy of Louis XIV's park at Versailles. The main building, erected in 1900-1902, bears clear evidence that the architect had traveled abroad a great deal. Minister Christian Thams, who commissioned Bårdshaug Manor as his private residence, was indeed an international person. Born in Trondheim in 1867, he moved to Orkdal at the end of the 19th century to take over Strandheim Mills, which had been established by his grandfather, Vilhelm A. Thams. Christian Thams trained as an architect in Zürich, Switzerland, and in 1888, he opened his own office in Nice, France. He quickly developed a following and was, among other things, responsible for the Norwegian pavilion at the Paris World Exhibition in 1889. At a similar exhibition in Chicago in 1908, he was foreman of the jury.

Christian Thams was not only an accomplished architect, he was also an inventive and industrious businessman. Eventually, he became Norway's first producer of prefabricated houses. When he took over Strandheim Mills in 1893, it was a lumber manufacturing business and the region's largest producer of crates. But Thams developed it further and began producing prefab houses. During a stay in Menton, in southern France, he experienced an earthquake and that's when the idea struck him. Why not build solid prefab log houses, specially constructed to be able to withstand earthquakes? As soon as he took over Strandheim, he put his idea into production, and his new project was an unqualified success. Prefabricated houses from Orkanger were exported to France, England, Belgium, Germany and Spain, and to South America, Africa and India as well.

Thams was also very farsighted technically – he built Orkdal's first electric power station at Skjenaldsfoss (waterfall). It supplied power to Strandheim Mills and to Bårdshaug Manor, which became the first private home in Orkanger with electricity. The station later was sold to Orkla Mine Corporation, today Orkla-Borregård, but in connection with the sale, Thams made Orkla sign a contract which guaranteed the manor 40 kilowatts of power free-of-charge forever. After the change in ownership, this

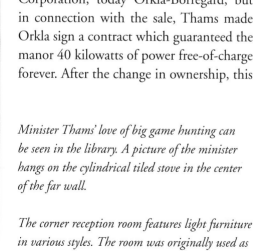

Minister Thams' love of big game hunting can be seen in the library. A picture of the minister hangs on the cylindrical tiled stove in the center of the far wall.

The corner reception room features light furniture in various styles. The room was originally used as a ladies' lounge (right).

contract was tried before a court of law. It was found valid, so Bårdshaug Manor still receives free electricity.

In addition to all his business activities, Christian Thams also held a number of official posts. He became Belgian consul in Trondheim in 1896, Belgian general consul in Norway in 1907, French vice consul in 1907, and plenipotentiary for Monaco after 1911.

Mining and the railroad

All the above aside, Christian Thams' lifework was the rebuilding of the copper mines at Løkken in Meldal, along with the first electrically powered railroad. The Thamshavn Railway, which went from Løkken to Orkanger, was opened by King Haakon VII in 1908. The two businesses, Orkla Mine Corporation and Christian Salvesen and Christian Thams Communications, became industrial success stories. The Swedish financier brothers, K.A. and Marcus Wallenberg, had an interest in the mines, and the development was so rapid that few could dream of such a thing at the time. One result is the Orkla concern we know today.

For a while, Christian Thams was administrative director of both corporations, but in 1910, he chose to step down because of disagreements with some of the other shareholders. He still had plenty to do. He had a home in Nairobi, where he also ran a mine. In addition, he did business in North Africa, Europe and America, and on top of all that, Prince Albert of Monaco appointed him as the official trade representative in Paris. He moved to the French capital in 1911 and resided there until he died in 1948.

A handsome manor

Bårdshaug Manor still stands as a shining monument to a man of the world, minister and great industrialist, Christian Thams. The manor is, for the most part, preserved exactly as it was during Thams' time. In addition to a large kitchen area and a sizable butler's pantry, the first floor features an exquisitely beautiful dining room in pine, designed especially for Bårdshaug Manor. The fantastic carving was done by two of the area's finest woodcarvers, Peder Olsen Sognli and John Graven, who spent two years working on the project. Wall to wall with the dining room is a garden room and a corner room. These were used as reception rooms for women guests at the manor, while the men usually retired to the library, also on the first floor. This room is furnished with trophies from Christian Thams' hobby: big game hunting. Here he assembled trophies from countless safaris in Africa, as well as from hunts closer to home.

Bårdshaug Manor was built for minister and industrialist Christian Thams. The main building was constructed in a variety of styles and is unique for its type in the country. It still has its original exterior from 1900-1904.

The second floor contains eight large guest bedrooms. The most beautiful are the bridal suite and the royal room, which acquired its name after King Oscar II stayed there in 1902, just after the house was finished. Christian Thams had a special bed carved for the visit. Later, it was used by the Prince of Monaco, Belgian King Leopold and our own King Haakon VII.

The bridal suite contains the hotel's finest furniture, in French Louis XVI style from around 1780.

The dining room is ready for any occasion when the table is set with a white damask tablecloth and the minister's own porcelain in the "straw pattern" from the Royal Danish Porcelain factory in Copenhagen (below).

From manor to hotel

After Thams died, the local authorities took over Bårdshaug Manor. Today, it is part of Bårdshaug Manor Hotel, which is owned and run by Marit Müller Lysholm and Gunnar Lysholm. Marit is the daughter of hotelier Alf Hugo Müller, who purchased Bårdshaug Manor in 1965. It was not an easy task to run a hotel with only eight guest rooms at a profit, so when Marit and Gunnar took over in 1979, they built a new, modern hotel building only 200 meters from the old manor. But it is still possible to stay in Thams' old residence. Just remember to ask for a room in the old building when you make your reservation.

The main building at Bårdshaug really looks like an old manor, even though it is not a noble residence, as use of the word manor is supposed to convey. It was built from 1900 to 1905 in several different older shapes and styles and looks like a manorhouse which has been extended and altered over a very long period of time. This type of stylistic combination, with built-in historical traditions, was not at all unusual in the decades around 1900, and examples can be found all over Europe. Bårdshaug features many old Norwegian shapes which have been combined to create a very distinctive building.

Norwegian elements were used frequently in the extensive production of pre-fabricated houses, manufactured by the contractor's firm at Strandheim in Orkanger. An excellent example from around the turn of the century is the little doll house in the yard which was inspired by old storehouses in the valleys of eastern Norway.

All these different elements are combined and unified by the architect-contractor, Christian Thams. He studied to become an architect in Zürich before he took over the family business as a manufacturer and entrepreneur. With Bårdshaug, he created a specific rooms in a particular major style which could be associated with the purpose of the room. This was done at Bårdshaug, where it remains to this day. The dining room features Neo-Baroque furniture, with characteristic high-backed chairs and a buffet with rich carvings and powerful curved cornices. The ladies' salon is furnished in French Rococo and Louis XVI styles, which were considered feminine, while the library was furnished in a more masculine style, with hunting trophies and dark mahogany furniture in the dark interior. The room could use some comfortable leather armchairs, but one can still imagine the scent of cigars.

A manor in many styles

The long and narrow central wing is clearly modeled after the traditional Trøndelag longhouse decorated with pilasters, or flat imitation columns, on the facades. Crosswise additions at both ends create a courtyard. On the garden side, there is a veranda with Neo-Classical style columns dating from around 1800, while the corner bay window is crowned with a Baroque style tower roof as often seen during the 1600's and 1700's. In many places, the walls are decorated with an early 18th-century type of carved vine leaves of which eventually became very popular in Norwegian folk art.

The stone corner tower on one side serves as a landmark. It looks like the remains of an old fort. It is built in a rounded medieval style with carved decorative banding in a zigzag pattern along the openings which are called Norman (after the Normans of Normandy and England in the 11th and 12th centuries.) When Bårdshaug was built, researchers thought that this style had developed from the wooden building tradition the Vikings brought to Normandy around 900 A.D. The door handles and the railing on the tower balcony feature Viking-inspired Nordic ornament combined with some Art Nouveau shapes which were popular when Bårdshaug was built. A painted brown veranda or gallery in dragon style, inspired by old Norwegian log houses, extends from the tower. It is richly decorated with carvings inspired by the intertwining dragons of stave church decoration. The more rustic gallery originally was meant to be another Viking-influenced element. Such national,

Gentlemen enjoy refreshments in the garden on the occasion of the opening of the Thamshavn Railroad in 1908. King Haakon VII stands at the center of the picture. Photograph: Property of Bårdshaug Manor.

framework around his life, which gave the impression of both riches and traditions.

The interiors are just as impressive as the exterior. Fine furniture and decorations are combined with antiques and newer furniture, which Thams had made in the different historical revival styles which were popular in the decades around the turn of the century. At that time, it was popular to furnish

The lamps and chandeliers deserve special mention. Those in the dining room are in the Baroque style as is everything else in the room, but otherwise there is an exquisite collection in Art Nouveau, which was the height of fashion during the early years of electricity. Some of the furnishings which are too fragile for daily use have been moved to the little museum in the cellar.

Financed by the King of Hawaii

An old gravel road
over a marsh.
Two slanting posts.
Then the forest opens
onto a farm.
With grassy mounds
and ancient birch
Here is a view over the water,
the hills, peaks and bogs.

Here lies Lisbetsæter
old and proud
against a broad sky.
And around the "woman" of
the farmyard
stand Lunden - Granly,
Grindstua - Lia and others.
At Lisbetsæter it's good
to be alive!

kw.

This is the way a poet describes the magnificent setting of the old majestic log building which is Lisbetsæter Guesthouse today. Dr. Eyvind Kraft built the "woman" here, 300 meters above sea level at Skaun, 45 kilometers south of Trondheim and 10 kilometers from Orkanger, over 100 years ago. Back then, it was called Lisbetsæter Sanitarium and Hydrotherapy Spa, but in that same building, Dr. Kraft treated Europe's aristocracy and upper classes for the great scourge of the day. Tuberculosis was fought in the clean, fresh air, surrounded by forests and the grand expanse of Trøndelag, and with a wonderful view of Vinås Lake.

But let's not get ahead of the events. This natural gem had been discovered many hundreds of years earlier, and in the Middle Ages, there was a mountain dairy farm at Lisbetsæter. Then it was called Byasætra and belonged to By farm in Skaun. But soon there was a need for land, and in 1610, there was a permanent dwelling at the old mountain farm. According to a land register from 1683, the farm was owned by Rein monastery in Rissa. Later, the property was transferred to the Danish-Norwegian king, first to Frederik IV and later to Christian VI. In a new land register from 1726, the name Lisbetsæter was used for the first time. It is uncertain how the farm got its name. According to legend, it was called after Lisbet Nypan, who was burned at the stake in 1670, but it is more likely that the name comes from the widow Lisbet, who ran the farm from 1623 onwards. When Christian VI died in 1746, the property was purchased by Meldalen Works, later called Løkken Copper Works. In 1820, it was sold to Ole Olsen Kuvåssæter, usually called just "Sætermannen" (the farmer).The Olsen family were the last residing farmers at Lisbetsæter. Some decades later, when Ole's son Ingebrigt bought a farm at Fokseth, he sold the place to Dr. Eyvind Kraft, whose endeavors made this remote but beautiful place in south Trøndelag known far beyond Norway's borders.

Doctor and adventurer

Dr. Eyvind Kraft was the son of Isak and Kathinka Kraft, who moved from eastern Norway to Orkdal when Isak became district magistrate there in 1867. They had four children, but Eyvind was the only son. He finished medical school in 1979 and moved to Hof in Solør, where he practiced medicine for a short time. Then, the young adventurer signed on with a sailing ship as ship's doctor across the Atlantic to America. He eventually established his own practice there, but he was not one to settle down. He traveled to Hawaii, where he became personal physician to the King. On this exotic island in the Pacific Ocean, Eyvind Kraft was regarded as a new and exciting addition. Through his position as the royal physician, he had access to court circles, and soon, one of the princesses fell in love with him and wanted to marry him. But the King did not want a Norwegian son-in-law. In order to get rid of him, he paid Eyvind to leave the island. And so, it is told, the adventurous doctor returned to Norway and Orkdal as a man of means.

There is a wonderful view over Vinås lake, forest, mountain, and the hazy distance from the second-story gallery - the wonderful landscape that inspired the building of a sanitarium at Lisbetsæter.

The interiors are simple and rugged with untreated wood and visible log walls. The furniture dates from the hotel's period as a sanitarium.

The main building at Lisbetsæter is in the style of the long farm buildings of the Trøndelag region. After additions were constructed at each end, the verandas now seem like galleries (left).

"Lisbetsæter Sanitarium and Hydrotherapy Spa"

Once home again, Eyvind Kraft took over Lisbetsæter in 1886. In America, he had acquired new information about the treatment of tuberculosis, and he now wanted to build a treatment and rest home for those suffering from the illness. He tore down some old farm buildings and moved others, and he started building Lisbetsæter Sanitarium and Hydrotherapy Spa. In 1890, Kraft's lifework was ready for guests. The main building stood, as it does today, on the crest of a hill with a panorama to the south, surrounded by 11 small, red houses. It could house up to 120 guests at a time, and it soon became a popular spa for rich and famous Europeans with tuberculosis. Swedes, Danes, Finns, Russians and Englishmen found their way to Lisbetsæter, and in the summer months especially, it was a very international place. It was not at all unusual to see elegant four-wheel carriages with two pairs of shining, well-groomed horses and driver pull up at Lisbetsæter. The passengers could easily be counts and barons. Even Prince Albert of Monaco came here to enjoy the clean, fresh and life-giving air in these beautiful natural surroundings. Everything was arranged for the guests to have a successful stay. They could take warm and cold baths in a separate spa. The bowling pavilion was built for more

social pleasures, and ten kilometers of gravel walking paths were laid out. Other buildings were constructed, and a seven-seat outhouse was given the name "Endeli" (a play on words which meant both "finally" and "seat in the mountains"). Kraft supplied rowboats at the nearby lakes, and he made a private beach at Bya pond, right by Lisbetsæter. It is still in use today.

Many new owners

In 1891, Eyvind married Anna Birch, and they had two children, daughter Astrid, born in 1893, and son Reidar, born in 1899. Eyvind Kraft died the following year, only 47 years old. His widow continued to run the sanitarium for a few years, but in 1907, she sold it to a lumber merchant in Trondheim, Mikael Øyen. He, in turn, sold it in 1911, and the property as it is today was sold to brothers Olaf and Hjalmar Solem, while the forest was sold separately. The Solems were not interested in running the place, so Lisbetsæter changed owners shortly thereafter. Trondheim's Junior Chamber of Commerce, now called Trondheim Business and Office, purchased the property in 1918, and the venerable sanitarium became a guesthouse and resort, open to both members of the association and to others. Rates were supposed to be low, so that everyone could afford a stay at Lisbetsæter. This created con-

stant financial problems, but thanks to bazaars, lotteries, and the members' own volunteer work, the association was able to retain Lisbetsæter for 20 years. In 1938, however, they decided to sell the property. Seven members of the association formed the Lisbetsæter Corporation, which assumed management of the place. One of these members, Yngve Gulbrandsen, was manager until 1958. In our own time, Johan P. Rønne is probably the man most often connected with Lisbetsæter. He took over after Gulbrandsen and was manager for nearly 30 years. After a while, it was no longer profitable, and in the middle of the 1960's, the guesthouse was closed. The small houses were leased as cabins, as they are today, and the main building was shut. And decay set in...

Back to its earlier glory

At the end of the 1980's, the present owners, descendants of the last two shareholders from 1938, decided to reopen the guesthouse. With help from the authorities and considerable voluntary work,

The old kitchen is simple and beautiful, with wide wooden paneling on the walls, while the interior is an unusually fresh blue with a lovely patina that comes from many years of use. The old wood stove is used for preparing hearty Norwegian peasant fare.

restoration was started, and in 1990, the main building was re-opened as a restaurant. The sale of food and drink helped finance further remodeling, and in 1992, the main building was finally ready to resume its former role as a guesthouse. Today, the "woman" of the farmyard is painted white with green trim framing the long galleries and the beautiful gingerbread verandas. Little has been changed since Dr. Kraft's time. Inside, the large two-story building houses a kitchen, dining room, lounges and a ballroom on the first floor, while the second features nine charming guest rooms. Both lounges and bedrooms are simply but pleasantly furnished, with furniture from the time the house was built over 100 years ago.

This is not a modern luxury hotel. Now as earlier, it is the beauty of nature, clean, fresh air and excellent opportunities for hunting and fishing which attract guests to Lisbetsæter.

Lisbetsæter has a history as a mountain dairy farm, but it has a completely different function today. Dr. Kraft planned his sanitarium with a central main building surrounded by smaller villas. According to the opinion of the day, tuberculosis patients needed clean, dry air, the reason most sanitariums were built at high places. Dr. Kraft had supposedly learned a new method of curing the illness. Patients were supposed to get masses of fresh air but

furniture is in a combination of Biedermeier and Renaissance Revival. Other furnishings in wood or cane, light enough to be moved around or out onto the veranda.

Eventually 12-15 smaller villas and cabins in different shapes were constructed around the main building. Families could rent them and bring their servants and whatever else wealthy bourgeoisie had with them in those days. It is said that two of these

wealthy cityfolks who came to enjoy the view. A staircase up to the second floor is out on the veranda, which not only saved space inside, but it also made renting the house more flexible. With the staircase outside, the house could be rented to more than one family at a time, according to need and budget.

More than just the buildings have been renovated at Lisbetsæter. The grounds had begun to grow wild. Earlier, there were animals grazing and farmers

A continental cultural idiom in humble format

they were to avoid the sun. This has been used as an explanation for the many verandas on the different buildings. Such verandas, though, were featured in much of the architecture of that time.

The buildings at Lisbetsæter have been remodeled over the years. An old photograph shows the main building just after it was erected. It had unpaneled log walls, but probably it was intended to be paneled – the building had to settle a few years before panels could be added. This was often the case with buildings made of notched logs. This building had two-story verandas around all four sides. The building it-self was as long as the present gallery and still serves as the core of the main building. It hardly bears any traces of modern architecture of its time. It was more in the local tradition, with long and somewhat narrow buildings. The verandas made it both unusual, beautiful and sophisticated, compared to what was normal in the district.

In a photo from around 1920, the first floor veranda on one gable wall is glassed in, and the first smaller annex has been added on the other side. Later, the verandas on both short sides were removed and the building was extended with a wide addition. Because of this, the earlier verandas on the long sides appear as the recessed galleries still visible today. Around 1920, the ballroom was added.

The lounges and guest bedrooms are still the original, with a somewhat rustic look, which was the norm on the farms of the district at the time. Both common rooms and bedrooms are equipped with the furniture of the day. Some of the upholstered

were gifts from Minister Thams, produced at M. Thams & Co. at Orkdalsøra, one of the country's larger producers of lumber and prefabricated buildings. Around 1900, this firm exported houses such as these all over the world. It was normal to give such villas and annexes names which were both exotic and poetic. At Lisbetsæter, they were named after their locations, such as Lia (Hillside) and Grindstua (Gate House). Some were built in variations of the "Swiss style" and many have been altered through the years.

Vestheim, a double house, has two verandas modeled after forms derived from old storehouses of the type found in Setesdal, Telemark and other valleys in eastern Norway. This can be seen in the heavy turned posts and in the arches between the posts on the second floor, which were inspired by such store-house galleries. But as verandas, they have a more open design, which was new at the time, adapted for

Originally, the main building at Lisbetsæter was surrounded by two stories of verandas on all four sides. After a while, they were enclosed in glass to make them warmer, and additions were begun at both ends. This photograph from around 1920 shows how the building looked after the first, smaller changes.
Photograph: Private collection.

planting crops and clearing trees on the land. And here, there were trails for guests. When left untouched, such things disappear. Now, this aspect has become more important in cultural preservation. With support from the Ministry of Agriculture, trails and meadows around Lisbetsæter have been cleared, and today, the grounds are well maintained.

Lisbetsæter stands as witness to a bygone era. At the same time, the complex is a gentle reminder of far off and more famous spas and resorts, such as Karlsbad, Wiesbaden and Deauville. Thanks to the surrounding countryside, the humble format and the relatively simple building style, the mood is completely different. It is a Norwegian — one can even say local — rural version of a continental cultural idiom.

HOTEL UNION
Øye

A Belle Époque castle in the Sunnmøre Alps

Right in the heart of the Sunnmøre Alps is the little town of Øye. It is often called Norway's best kept secret, for it is tucked away between tall mountains innermost in Norangfjord, a sidearm of the better known Hjørundfjord.

As with so many naturally beautiful places in this lengthy land, the area around Norangfjord was "discovered" already when

the first tourists begin to come to Norway at the end of the last century. They were most often adventurers, explorers and mountain climbers. Sometimes they knew only one sentence in Norwegian, but they used it often. "Er det fjeld bestiget?" "Has this mountain been climbed?" These words were said frequently as tourists landed at Øye and were impressed by the majestic mountains, with Slogen and Smørskredtind as solid landmarks. And the local drivers at quayside always shook their heads in the negative as they respectfully looked over to the mountains, where they themselves fetched lost sheep down from tiny ledges every autumn. Novelty and pioneer interest had to be maintained!

Even though these first tourists were in constant search of the wild and uncivilized, they were not interested in simple accommodation. No, they wanted good food, comfortable beds and fine, vintage Port served on the terrace where they could enjoy the view of the "wilderness". And to satisfy these needs, it was decided to build a modern hotel all the way in the nearly hidden fjord arm in Sunnmøre.

From bankruptcy to consul to church

A corporation led by Director Adolf Schelderup financed the construction of Hotel Union at Øye and Hotel Union in Geiranger. Building both hotels at the same time was too great a project, and even before the beautiful wooden castle at Øye was finished, the company went bankrupt.

But luckily, the wonderful building, which had been prefabricated in Trondheim and shipped by boat to Norangfjord, did

When the current owners took over the hotel, it was stripped of its original furnishings. Now it is furnished with a successful combination of the old and the new.

The old stairs go from the reception area up to the guest rooms on the second and third floors. These interiors are among the best preserved at the hotel (right).

not stay empty for long. That same year, the Norwegian consul in Spain bought it, and the hotel opened as planned, in June, 1891. Konsul Tonning had neither the time nor the possibility to the place himself. His sister and her husband, Peter Stub, were responsible for running one of Norway's most modern hotels at the time. The consul himself visited regularly, often bringing with him a large group of Spanish friends, even after he later sold the hotel.

The new hotel soon became a popular gathering place for royalty, aristocrats and other wealthy people who could afford to travel in those days. Kaiser Wilhelm II of Germany visited the hotel many times, and on July 22, 1896, the King of Sweden and Norway, Oscar II visited with a party of 12. In 1906, King Haakon, Queen Maud and Crown Prince Olav docked in Norangfjord and visited the hotel during their travels through the country following the Coronation. Queen Wilhelmina and Crown Princess Juliana, later Queen of the Netherlands, were also loyal guests at the hotel, as were famous authors, such as Karen Blixen and Bjørnstjerne Bjørnson.

In 1913, Consul Tonning decided to sell the hotel. At the same time, Martin Laurits Dahl, originally from Geiranger but a resident of the United States for 18 years, decided to move back to the old country. He had worked in hotels in America for many years and had also spent a year in Germany. He decided to return to Ørsta in the spring of 1913, because his wife Birgitte was expecting a child. On their way home, they stayed one night at Hotel Union in Øye, and they had a conversation with Consul Tonning. He was looking for a buyer and offered the couple the hotel with "all rights and glories." Martin and Birgitte accepted the offer on the spot, and Hotel Union became the family business and remained so for 68 years. When Martin Laurits Dahl died in 1954, his son Karl and wife Aslaug took over running the hotel. They continued until Karl became ill in 1972. Then it was leased to Ingvald Rørnes who was responsible for the business until 1976, when Aslaug and Karl's son, Leif Dahl, took over. In 1981, the hotel was sold out of the family to Ørsta Free Church, which ran it as a combination hotel and course center until 1989.

Return to glory

Now, the venerable hotel fell upon less secure times. Many years had passed since it had been fixed up, and maintenance had not been a priority, either. The building was totally dilapidated on the outside, and all the furnishings inside were completely rundown. The wallpaper hung in shreds, and the once beautiful lounges were filled with worn-out post-war furniture. Should the building be demolished, or was there perhaps someone "crazy" enough to take on the challenge of restoring it?

The functional extension of the lounges gracefully turns the corner of the older, richly decorated, wooden building.

The many windows in the lounge makes the room light and airy.

There was indeed. Physiotherapist and acupuncturist Per Ola Ratvik from Ålesund had driven past many times and fell completely in love with the old wooden building. So when the Free Church finally decided to sell in 1989, he bought it. Even though most people thought he would never make it, he was determined that Hotel Union at Øye would rise again in all its former glory.

Per Ola Ratvik recruited three local shareholders, farmers and fur farmers Idar Nordang and Johan Øye, along with researcher Ivar Lødemæl. Together they started on the laborious task of restoring the hotel. First, they removed all rubbish from the building. One of the few things which stayed was a large rock on the third floor. Although the hotel site is not avalanche-prone, it has felt pressure from powerful Slogen. In 1940, German bombers came down the Norang valley to bomb the Norwegian tanker "Beaufort" anchored in the fjord. One bomb fell high up the side of the mountain, and some large rocks were loosened. One of these came hurling through the air and through the roof of the hotel,

The guest bedrooms are tastefully and individually decorated. Most have new canopy beds made to old designs.

where it crashed down onto and partially into the third floor, where it has remained.

Today, the owners admit that they did not realize completely the extent of the task when they began the restoration, and that it cost them blood, sweat and tears. But they succeeded. Today, the hotel is just like the original Belle Epoque hotel, both inside and out. Per Ola Ratvik has scoured all of Europe to find antiques for the beautiful rooms, so visitors can have a good idea of how it must have looked years ago. Spending a summer evening in one of the lounges at Hotel Union is like traveling back in time 100 years. The open window with white lace curtains frames the beautiful, untouched landscape outside. The scent of grass and wild flowers wafts in along with the light rushing sound of nearby waterfalls. The soft conversation of the guests blends with the tones of Grieg's music. The flames in the fireplace give the room a glow, and the candles in the large silver candelabra flicker and cast an special glow over the lounge. Yes, the new owners of Hotel Øye have succeeded. And they were repaid for all that hard work in 1993, when Queen Sonja chose to bring guests here during the Royal couple's Silver Wedding journey to western Norway. At last, Europe's royalty had returned to the wonderful Belle Époque castle at Norangfjord.

When Hotel Union was dedicated in 1891, it had no history as a commercial center or guesthouse, as did so many hotels in Vestlandet. It was the beauty of the scenery and the increasing tourism of the modern age which provided the basis for its construction. A corporation started it all and had the building delivered prefabricated from M. Thams & Co. in Trondheim. The result was, architecturally speaking, one of the most varied and richly designed wooden hotels from the last part of the 19th century.

The identity of the architect is uncertain, but it may have been Christian Thams, who had trained as an architect in Zürich and who had just assumed leadership of the lumber firm. He had also designed a small wooden house in the same style which was

When the Union Hotel was built in 1891, it had even greater variation in verandas and decorative gables than what remains today. The photograph was taken at the beginning of the 20th century when the building was still in its original form.
Photograph: Private collection.

New owners thoroughly renovated the hotel for its 100-year jubilee. The exterior was repaired,

Richness of shapes, Belle Époque and nostalgia

awarded a medal at the 1889 World Exhibition in Paris. It was purchased as the office building for the Eiffel Tower, which had been erected for the same exhibition, and which was supposed to be demolished 20 years later.

In its early days, Hotel Union was even more strongly influenced by contemporary wooden architecture than it appears today. There were open verandas in fantastic beam constructions the entire length of the first floor on the two main facades of the dining and reception room wing. At the end of the main wall of the guest bedroom wing, there was also a large dormer with a rich beam construction in an elegant arch with decorative inserts, in addition to decorative gables which are still preserved on the main wing. In 1926, the large dormer was removed when the roof was raised to make space for new guest bedrooms in the former attic. Two small roof towers were added at that time. The two dormers on the front facing the fjord and the beautiful gable on the main wing, with its jigsaw decorations with rosettes and tendrils, still preserve some of the abundance of decoration on the original hotel exterior. It is common to call such shapes "Swiss style," but in this case, it is far more correct to speak of historicism in wooden architecture with shapes drawn from many sources, including German half-timber traditions and English roof constructions from the Middle Ages.

The hotel was managed enthusiastically for a long time and modernized as time went by. In 1937, the verandas in front of the lounges were replaced by an addition in front of the dining room and reception rooms. With its flat roof, curved corners and bands of windows across the facade, it is typical of 1930's functionalism. It works well with the old building, in spite of the stylistic differences. The interior of the hotel was also refurbished and modernized frequently. By the beginning of the 1980's, there was not much left of the earlier details and original inventory.

and parts of the interior were restored to their original appearance. In addition, many new elements were added, with romantic details and stenciled decoration which, to a great degree, are in line with what was popular during the time around 1900. The chairs in the dining room have a long history at the hotel, while the remaining furniture is mostly new, but in a variety of older styles. The wicker furniture in the smoking salon is typical of that used in many European hotels in the period before the First World War.

Today's historical furnishings and ambiance are the result of an effort to recreate an atmosphere of a time long gone, with nostalgia and references to the "Belle Époque" period before World War I and to the hotel's famous guests of the day. The staircase area is probably the best preserved part of the interior, but the exterior of the building is close to the original, except for lesser additions constructed in 1926 and 1937.

VISNES HOTEL

Stryn

Where fjords, mountains, and glaciers meet

The beautiful agricultural area of Stryn, at heart of Nordfjord, is one of western Norway's biggest tourist destinations. Stryn is the place where fjords, mountains, and glaciers meet, and where the splendid and varied landscape entices many tourists who are sports and fresh air enthusiasts. Some come to fish salmon in the renowned Stryn River, while others come to wander along the glaciers or hike in the mountains. Many visitors come to ski – even in the summer. Tystig Glacier has Europe's best summer snow, and at Stryn Summer Ski Center there's a 975-meter-long ski lift up the glacier, and once there, a 775-

meter-long glacier ski tow awaits. Those interested in alpine skiing can choose among several different runs, the longest one, 2100 meters, with a drop of 518 meters. There are also many kilometers of well-prepared rambling and cross-country skiing trails on the glacier plateau.

Visnes Hotel, in the center of Stryn, is the best reason to visit the village. Sheltered by mighty mountains, with a view over the fjord stands the old, white wooden building as it has for close to 150 years. Over the years, the building has been expanded and extended several times, but it has yet to lose its charm. Visnes Hotel is still a peaceful and cozy oasis for travelers.

From generation to generation
Today, Kristin Visnes runs the old family hotel in Stryn. Her great-great-grandfather, Anton Arnesen Visnes, built it in 1850. Since then, the building has been handed down in the family from generation to generation. Kristin took over after her father

Visnes hotel was built in stages. The original building from the 1800's was presumably built into the closest part with the old stairway in front. Today's large facade with its two gables its the result of additions in the 1920's and 1930's.

The veranda offers a protected view of the fjord and the surrounding landscape (right).

A mahogany-stained birch bookcase from the end of the 1800's and two distinctive chairs from the time around the First World War can be found in the lounge.

in 1986. At that time, it had been closed for 29 years. In the past, the hotel's grounds had stretched all the way down to the sea. The white wooden building was surrounded by a large, delightful garden with quantities of fruit trees and its own beach. The grounds were fantastic! But in 1957, the municipality decided to expropriate much of the grounds to construct a road and build new houses. Kristin's father gave up and closed the hotel.

The agony of the decision

When it became Kristin's turn to take over the property, she agonized over the decision. She lived and worked in Oslo. Should she give up a well-paid secretarial job and move to Stryn to run a hotel? She knew that the hotel trade was no easy business, and besides that, the hotel needed a good deal of renovation after having been closed for almost 30 years. At the same time, she had been born and raised at the hotel and wanted to return to Stryn, where she had roots. What should she do?

The hostess herself, Kristin Visnes, loves the large, old fashioned kitchen. She prepares all the food from scratch. Traditional Norwegian food is the hotel's specialty.

The fine Renaissance Revival buffet from the end of the 1800's is painted to imitate exotic wood (right).

The large and airy dining room is blue and white, with white lace curtains at the windows.
The dining room is set for dinner, which at Visnes is always a three-course meal..

She finally took a risk on the family business. For the first three years, she lived in Stryn during the summer and in Oslo during the winter. In order to keep everything going financially, she needed extra income and therefore alternated between working at the hotel and being a secretary.

Soon, the tourists rediscovered this charming little hotel, and in 1989, Kristin moved back to Stryn for good. Since then, the old building has taken up all her time and all her money. Slowly but surely, she has been able to renovate the dining room, the lounges and some of the guest rooms. Some things still remain to be done, but Kristin knows just how she wants it, and she is willing to wait, so that everything can be done properly. She wants to return the hotel to its former glory.

A home away from home

Visnes Hotel has just 12 guest bedrooms. Kristin sees this as an advantage. She wants her guests to experience the hotel as a home away from home. And that includes home cooking. Every morning, the tables in the breakfast room are beautifully set, and the guest rise to the smell of homemade bread and rolls, homemade orange marmalade, and fresh strawberry jam. Every day at 5, coffee and homemade cakes are served in the cozy sitting room. In the evening, the door is opened to the large, airy dining room, where guests enjoy freshly caught salmon or halibut, deer, stew, and grandmother's prune dessert...Is it any wonder that guests return to Visnes Hotel year after year?

The oldest hotel at Visnes, similar to so many other guesthouses and hotels in western Norway from the middle of the 19th century, was a one-story building in the typical western Norwegian building tradition of the time. Around the turn of the century, it had a gabled facade with a two-story veranda projecting from the middle of the long wall. It looks as if this building was extended to two complete floors with a high attic around 1921, after its competitor, Hotel Central, on the neighboring lot, closed its doors during the First World War. The addition was given a long veranda in front of the first floor, and in the middle, the old veranda was extended upward three floors under a pointed gable. The building was strongly marked by the "Swiss style" and the Gothic Revival, which was now regarded as old-fashioned in more central places. A description from 1922 notes that owner Kristian Visnes, who had

Visnes hotel began small, as shown on this 1906 postcard. It was a typical Nordfjord house from the last half of the 1800's, but the veranda signals that the place took in paying guests. This house was obviously incorporated into the 1921 expansion, but the veranda, with its steep stairs, still remains. Photograph: Private collection.

Genuine and colorful

a farm there, lived in the building with his family, where they ran a hotel in the summer months. The first floor contained dining room, lounge, kitchen, office and two rooms, while the second floor contained eight bedrooms.

In 1932, there was not supposed to be much traffic at the hotel, but only five years later, it was extended to the south in the same style it had been given in 1921. The dining room was built, and the second gabled projection and veranda were added to the main facade. Inside are details and furnishings from many of the building's historic periods. The plywood panels covering some walls were considered very modern in the 1920's and 1930's and date from the last period of construction.

Visnes Hotel is not as old as it looks. But it was closed from 1957 to 1986 and avoided additions during a time when the original style was hardly appreciated. Many such hotels were ruined by thoughtless modernization and incongruous additions. Now, the old style and atmosphere are being preserved by a hostess with a great sense of color, who also understands the original intentions of the place.

GLOPPEN HOTEL
Sandane

Salmon as the basis for life

Gloppen Hotel is located in Sandane, innermost in Gloppenfjord, surrounded by wild and beautiful western Norway. The old white wooden main building looks like a majestic manor surrounded by a large and beautiful garden. It overlooks the river, which, in its time, was the reason such a hotel was built here. Fishermen from around the world come to this idyllic place in Nordfjord to cast their lines for salmon and trout. In 1904, Gloppen was listed in the English guidebook "Salmon Fishing in Norway" as one of the best fishing spots in the country. But the English salmon lords had discovered Gloppen long before that.

In Great Britain, salmon fishing was a luxury limited to the few owners of enormous estates and the nobility, while in Norway, anyone could fish in a good river, as long as he paid a few crowns to a hospitable farmer. As early as 1872, Sandane landowners realized that the Gloppen River could provide them with a handsome income, so they began to rent out fishing rights. And sports fishermen came in droves – which, of course, prompted the need for hotels at Sandane.

From coaching inn to guesthouse

Since 1846, there has been a hotel on the site where Gloppen Hotel now stands. The first 20 years, there was just a simple inn, but in 1866, Joakim E. Sivertsen received permission to run a country store at:

"Sanden in Gloppen parish, Sønd and Nordfjord bailiff's office, Northern Bergenshus district with obligation to:

1. maintain a guesthouse, but without the right to serve liquor or any mixed drink.

2. if demanded, to take over maintaining a courtroom for a fee as decided or to be decided, and to perform duties as shipping agent for steamship in the service of the post office for a fee as decided by the post office.

3. to pay a yearly fee of 8 spesidaler to the National Treasury. Moreover, on condition:
   a) that he shall keep the place stocked with necessary wares.
   b) that he shall keep the guesthouse in good condition and for a reasonable sum supply travelers with necessary and good accommodation as well as food and drink, the latter in accordance to the lawmakers' decision regarding restriction. Or loss of license will result."

Among lords and emigrants

The new guesthouse at Sandane was a rousing success and soon needed to expand. In 1890, Sivertsen built the first part of what is now Gloppen Hotel. Back then, though, he called the hotel after himself. Sivertsen's Hotel quickly became a natural gathering place for the English salmon lords, but just as important for business at the turn of the century was the steady stream of Norwegian emigrants to America. Cunard Line, the steamship company, had a ticket office at the hotel, and for many Norwegian emigrants, Sivertsen's Hotel was their last stop in the old country.

Business boomed, and by 1925, another addition was needed. The old hotel was extended in the same style as the part of the building which today houses the beautiful lounges and reception rooms. According to the standards of the day, it was a modern hotel, with both running water and electricity. The hotel's most successful period was from this time until the Second World War.

Over the years, many a salmon fisherman has enjoyed a large four-course lunch in this beautiful old room. Today, the menu features fish and shellfish soup, salmon fricassee with coriander sauce, reindeer filet with onions glazed with red wine and port wine sauce, followed by cheesecake garnished with exotic fruits and blackberry sauce.

The traditional Sandane hotel specializes in gourmet food made from fresh Norwegian ingredients. Salmon is, of course, a regular feature on the menu.

Gloppen Hotel's symmetrical and monumental facade is the result of several enlargements. The left part of the hotel is the eldest (right).

The three-course menu served every night at Gloppen Hotel is an experience in itself.

In one of the sitting rooms is a grand piano and a Norwegian Neo-Classical bureau in mahogany-stained birch from the beginning of the 19th century (left).

New owners – old traditions

During the 1980's, the Sivertsen family withdrew and the hotel was made into a corporation. New owners and new bankruptcies followed, until K. Strømnes Salmon Breeders in Bremanger purchased it in 1988. They changed the name to Gloppen Hotel. The firm invested millions of crowns on rehabilitation of the venerable hotel, and today, guests can relive some of the atmosphere from the days when British salmon lords told their best fish stories over glasses of sherry in the lounge.

On December 1, 1994, the hotel changed owners once again. Dag Moen, who had managed the hotel for K. Strømnes, bought out his former employer and took over the hotel with his wife Irene. Both are interested in the history of the hotel and are always trying to journey back in time. This means taking care of old furniture and fixtures while restoring the old wooden building to make it look as it did in its glory days. In addition, the new owners are concentrating on maintaining Gloppen's reputation as a place for fine dining. Food meant a lot to sports fishermen in the hotel's early days. The men lived their own lives, with their own daily rhythm – early to rise and late to bed. But in the middle of the day, when the fish were not biting, they had ample time to

enjoy the pleasures of the table, with large four-course lunches and the best wines. These traditions are still prized at Gloppen Hotel. The kitchen specializes in gourmet food prepared with Norwegian ingredients, and the hotel has an excellent wine cellar. Even though times have changed, and winter guests now are mostly course and conference participants, salmon fishermen still dominate the summer season from the beginning of May through September. They still want good old-fashioned service, and they get it here. In 1996, the hotel acquired the fishing rights to Gloppen River. Yes, historic Gloppen Hotel is still an attractive salmon hotel.

The oldest part of the present hotel building was built in 1890 and replaced an even older house on the same site. The new hotel was built in paneled logs in two floors, 2/3 of the present wooden structure. The building was typical of medium-sized tourist hotels in western Norway at the time, with a simple rectangular layout, high ceilings and a steep roof. In front of the main entrance in the center was a three-story open veranda, in which the roof extended upwards in a high pointed gable. The steep roofs and pointed gables are typical stylistic characteristics of the Gothic Revival. This is also true for the pointed leaf shapes which decorate the gables and which earlier also could be found all over the veranda. This was altered around 1923, when the second and third floor verandas were enclosed and incorporated into new guestrooms. The kitchen and dining room, as well as some smaller rooms, were originally on the first floor, while there were 13 guest bedrooms on the second floor and five in the loft. During the earliest years of the hotel, there was a shop in the cellar.

Gothic Revival and handcarved furniture

In 1925, the hotel was extended lengthwise in the style of the earlier building as it was after the alteration two years previously. This addition also had a projection on the long side, but no veranda. In that way, today's powerful entrance facade was created. The desire to adapt new elements to suit the old was not a priority in 1970, when an addition was built in concrete on the back of the wooden building. It was designed with rectangular shapes, a flat roof and strips of windows across the facade. This occurred at a time when respect for the style of the old building was so low that one has to be thankful that it was left standing.

Inside, the hotel was simple and restrained, right from the beginning. Some older doors exhibit traditional shapes and monumental construction. In some

of the common rooms, the log walls are exposed, and the typical western Norwegian construction with walls of notched planks, which have been both sawed and planed flat, is plain to see. Walls in other lounges are covered with unpainted plywood panels where the seams are hidden by molding, which divides the walls into squares. During the 1920's and 1930's, this was considered new and modern and became a popular wall treatment. However, on a more traditional note, the hotel's fine collection of carved furniture in the dragon style, with tendrils, dragons and fantastic animals inspired by wood carvings of the Middle Ages, dates from the early part of this century.

The history of Gloppen Hotel tells of the development toward modern times. As late as 1915, a new

Sivertsen's new hotel building from 1890 forms the largest part of the surviving wooden building at Gloppen Hotel. Both veranda and gables are decorated with Gothic Revival style ornament. Photograph: J, Karlsen, 1905, National Office of Historic Monuments archives.

stable with room for eight horses was built. Only eight years later, the first garage was constructed. It was probably the first modern garage in Sandane, because there was a well in the floor for mechanics. At the same time, part of the stable was equipped for storing ice, which was cut during the winter and was used for cooling salmon and other foodstuffs. The old coaching inn really kept up with the times.

RØISHEIM HOTEL
Bøverdalen

A protected mountain paradise

Bøverdalen, with its magnificent and wild nature, is considered one of the most beautiful valleys in Norway. This is the setting for Røisheim Hotel, steeped in local tradition. Sognefjell (Mountain) Road, Norway's highest mountain pass, 1440 meters above sea level at its highest point, goes through the valley. The road extends from Lom to the peaks and glaciers of the Jotenheimen Mountains and continues down to Sognefjord, which extends far in under the mountains. Steep, green mountains line both sides of the narrow valley, and at the bottom, the Bøvre river twists in playful torrents. Røisheim Hotel, at 550 meters elevation, is the starting point for many exciting excursions. Hikes to the top of 2469-meter Galdhøpiggen and 17-meter lower Glittertind, along with skiing at Galdhøpiggen Summer Ski Center, are popular activities.

But most importantly, Røisheim Hotel attracts guests from near and far. Already in 1923, Røysheim Inn, as it was called in those days, was protected as an historic monument – not only because of the buildings and the complete country courtyard, but just as much because of the entire milieu, which has special historical value.

At Røisheim, guests are not just welcomed to a hotel, but also to a farm. And correctly so! Røisheim is really an old Gudbrandsdal two-courtyard farm. Once it was one of the valley's largest, with 40 employees. At that time, it was also North Gudbrandsdal's largest milk producer. Most of the 12 buildings which make up the hotel today date from the 18th century, but the oldest house on the courtyard is from the 16th century. The farm itself is much, much older. Røisheim has 17 old letters on parchment which prove that the Røisheim family has been on the farm since the 13th century. And no one knows how long they were there before that. Bøverdalen was settled early, and the use of "-heim" in the name means that Røisheim was cleared sometime between 1200 and 400 BC. The original farm was on the other side of the river, but it was destroyed by a landslide and later rebuilt where Røisheim Hotel is today.

Jotunheimen was "discovered"
The road over Sognefjell was opened in 1938 and replaced a simple dirt road. But the road through Bøverdalen is really an ancient royal road, the main road from Bergen to eastern Norway. Originally, it was just a pack trail for horses with sturdy legs, with rickety bridges over the worst stretches of river. The road was not at all safe, for there was the risk of being attacked by bad weather, snowstorms, bears and gangs of robbers. The farms were far apart in those days, so it was not unusual for travelers to stop at Røisheim. It was a place to rest and to wait for others to join the group. There was safety in numbers when setting out over the notorious mountain pass.

Røisheim became a heritage building in 1923. From its opening in 1858 to the present day, the milieu around the hotel has been carefully maintained.

The storehouse on the left is the oldest building at Røisheim, probably dating from the 1500's. (right).

The "discovery" of Jotenheimen really brought Røisheim into prominence. The mountains had been known to reindeer herders and fisherman since time immemorial, but in 1820, two young students, Carl Boeck and Baltasar Keilhau explored Jotenheimen. Here they found magnificent peaks, glaciers and passes. Through their enthusiastic descriptions, a "new" mountainous world became known far beyond the borders of the land. Students and other city folk headed for the mountains. In 1854, Steinar Sulheim, Ola Halvorsen Røisheim's neighbor, was the first man to reach the peak of Galdhøpiggen. Ten years later, it was Ola's turn, when he marked a new route to the highest mountain top in northern Europe directly from Røisheim. With that, life on the farm entered a new era. In 1858, Ola had taken over the inn and guesthouse from the neighboring farm at Hoft, and among the travelers, civil servants and salesmen, who had been the most frequent guests up to that time, there were now adventuresome city folks, eager to climb the mountains. There was a real invasion of eminent English mountain climbers, who went home and wrote enthusiastic books about their fantastic experiences.

A center for the sport of climbing

As time went by, there were more and more people at Røisheim. The years passed, and it became the European center for the sport of climbing. Ola himself became known as a tourist guide far beyond Norway's borders. The famous English mountaineer, William Slingsby, was the first to reach the top of Store Skagadølstind (Great Skagadøl Peak) on July 21, 1876. The instructor of many Norwegian climbers, he was a regular guest at Røisheim. Ola became his friend and mountain guide, and Slingsby's description of the farm and its owner gives an interesting picture of the conditions there during the second half of the 19th century:

"There is a farm with picturesque buildings grouped around a cortyard, at the foot of Galdhø, which separates the two mountain valleys, Bøverdalen and Visdalen. It is an excellent example of a large mountain farm, and the owner, Ola Røisheim, is both an accomplished mountain climber and an experienced guide in the Jotunheimen Mountains. I have spent many a lazy but happy days at Røisheim.

… the dwelling house and the many farm buildings balance on mountain rocks over a wild, narrow gorge out by the water, and the Bøver River snakes its way through. There are dozens of giant potholes. An old wooden bridge provides an extra painterly touch, and a channel fills a large wooden trough with water for washing day.

On the other side of the river are the potato fields, which are watered almost continuously. Streams of water spread into channels which extend in all directions down over the hillside. There are pools every so often, and by them stand the "water spreaders." Each one is armed with a wooden shovel, and with these, they spread water over the fields, even when it thunders.

Each morning, a groaning breakfast buffet is served in this part of the dining room.

Every evening, a flock of 60-70 goats come to the farm. Where they come from is a mystery. The milkmaids give them salt, and there is always a small battle among them in the courtyard. It is really only a friendly tussle, but they butt one another with a vengeance."

Artists come to Røisheim

There is no doubt that guests enjoyed staying at Røisheim. After the conquering of Jotenheimen began to die down, a new category of people, artists, started coming to the idyllic farm. Sensitive as they were, they soon became hopelessly enamored with both the picturesque farm, the magnificent surroundings and the friendly hospitality at Røisheim. They came and they stayed – and they returned year after year –the greatest painters, poets and composers of the age. Hans Gude, Edvard Grieg, Henrik Ibsen, Arne Garborg, Lars Jorde and Eilif Pettersen – to name a few. Artist Gerhard Munthe came for the first time in 1904 with Fritz Thaulow and was completely mesmerized. Up to his death in 1929, he spent 20 summers at Røisheim. He became close to the family there, and he described his last meeting with old Ola: "When I came out in the

Among the antiques at Røisheim are many lovely pieces decorated with the acanthus forms made famous in the valley.

At Røisheim, every meal is a celebration. Silver, crystal, and Porsgrunn porcelain's "straw pattern" are an essential part of the atmosphere (right).

morning, he stood there and chopped wood from great, solid pine logs – eager and interested. He had humor; he gave each log a name and talked with them as he chopped, while laughing in front of me. He, too, was a tough mountain pine tree."

Generation after generation

As time passed, new generations took over the old historic inn. Ola took over after Ola, and Ola after Ola. All the men at Røisheim were called Ola. The last Ola, old Ola's grandson, took over Røisheim in 1919. Along with his sisters, he continued to run the place in the same hospitable way as his predecessors, and with "Ola's happy, shining smile and intelligent eyes, Brit's motherly, kind care

The old schoolhouse has been converted into guest bedrooms with new beds in an old-fashioned style.

and Torø's home-cooked food made with love," the guests continued to flock to the historical inn in Bøverdalen. Many regular guests returned year after year. Even some royal guests found the way to Røisheim. Queen Wilhelmina of the Netherlands was here three times, her daughter Juliana two, Norway's then Crown Prince Olav came, as did Prince Oscar Bernadotte of Sweden.

The siblings ran the place for 45 years. They shut down the farm in 1955, but at the hotel, life was much the same. In 1964, Ola decided to retire. Signe Moland stepped in, so Røisheim stayed in the family. Her maternal grandmother was Ola's cousin.

Signe Moland was just as concerned with retaining the genuine hospitality and cozy atmosphere as her predecessor. She continued to run the place according to old traditions, but she also recognized that the complex had become rundown and old-fashioned. In close cooperation with the National Office of Historic Monuments, she began a comprehensive restoration, and for five years, major changes took place at Røisheim. A thousand square meters of roof were covered with turf, and all the buildings in the courtyard were renovated. The original milieu around the inn was recreated and preserved, while at the same time, much needed modern facilities were installed, so the hotel could be run profitably.

Fortunately, Signe managed the enormous task of changing a unique old inn into an equally unique jewel of Norwegian tourism today. She became a very popular hostess, and Røisheim's many loyal guests were sad when she decided to close the hotel and concentrate on a future as an attorney. Røisheim's 125-year history as a family-run inn and hotel were definitely over.

New owners – old traditions

The next two years, Røisheim was locked up tight, but in 1985, Signe Moland sold it to Wilfried Reinschmidt, originally from southern Germany, but now living in Oslo, and his wife, Unni (nee Haugen) from Lom. It was not a simple task for the couple to take over the renowned hotel in Bøverdalen. Four generations of hospitality and a reputation as one of Norway's coziest and unique hotels had to be retained and continued. But Unni and Wilfried soon showed that they could do it. At the same time as they sought to maintain the old traditions and to preserve the protected buildings and special atmosphere, they also gave the hotel a large dose of their own personality. Wilfried soon became renowned as a chef, and Røisheim became one of the country's best restaurants. But it was not just a case of dropping by for a good meal. Røisheim was Unni and Wilfried's home, and they wanted their guests to feel at home, too. They decided that the hotel should be reserved for guests only. People were no longer welcome just to look around, drink a cup of coffee or eat lunch. Guests at the hotel were to be left in peace! Not even disturbing elements such as TV, radio and newspapers were allowed. And the guests loved it. Once again, Røisheim was considered Norway's possibly most exclusive and distinctive hotel, and it soon became the destination of ambassadors, politicians, artists and other prominent people. But now, as earlier, the hotel's most important clientele were avid mountain wanderers who wanted to enjoy some time in such wonderful surroundings. The best known guest of all was, of course, Queen Sonja, who has returned frequently to Røisheim.

In 1995, Unni and Wilfried Reinschmidt decided to call it a day. After 10 years of running the hotel successfully, they were tired and wanted to enjoy life at a slower pace. Røisheim Hotel was sold to Røisheim Properties, a corporation owned by a group of private investors, mostly from Oslo. Christina and Lars Aanes, both chefs, were hired to run the hotel, and both owners and the new host and hostess are determined to manage it the way it has been done for close to 150 years. Røisheim Hotel in Bøverdalen will remain a protected mountain paradise in the future, as well.

To a great degree, Røisheim has retained its original building structure as an old farm in upper Gudbrandsdal in spite of its many years as a hotel. Even though many old barns and stables are gone, there is still a clear impression of the valley's typical courtyard style with many houses grouped around two square courtyards: the inner one with dwellings and storehouses and the outer courtyard with the barns and stables, where previously there were additional buildings for other farm animals.

The complex has been extended to accommodate growing numbers of travelers since 1858, when the farm became an inn. New buildings have been carefully fitted into the old plan, with its brown log

Ready for walking in the mountains – the men with staffs and the women with backpacks and parasols. The photograph was taken before 1895 and shows many of the buildings still standing today. On the left is Veslestugu with two storehouses behind. The middle construction has since become the bridal attic. An addition was built onto the main building in the 1860's, and behind it stands the old main building, which was demolished in 1920 and replaced with the current dining room and kitchen wing. Photograph: National Office of Historic Monuments archives.

Brown log buildings and acanthus leaves

houses with turf roofs. The building traditions of Gudbrandsdal are still the rule here.

The development of the complex can be followed from the 1860's to the present through fire insurance appraisals. The first new house for travelers was built in 1868, maybe even earlier. The old farmhouse was a two-story log building, and the new one, erected close by, now the eastern part of the main building, had the same type of construction. This addition still stands, with its open gallery facing the courtyard. From the beginning, it contained a hall against the old house, and on the first floor, a lounge, a smaller room and a pantry. On the second floor was a room with many beds and a large and a small guest bedroom. Just before 1920, the old farmhouse was torn down and replaced with what today is the dining room and kitchen.

In addition to the main building, the 1868 farm included a large number of other buildings for both people and animals. Many of them were considered old, even then, and most are still standing:

Veslestugu (little cottage) on one floor east of the courtyard. Two **storehouses** on the upper side of the courtyard. The smaller is thought to date from the 18th century, while the larger may date as far back as the 1500's. **Aurbua**, on the western side of the courtyard, was built in the 18th century and

originally had animals in the first floor and a sleeping loft above. Now it has guest bedrooms on both floors. The first floor of the **stable** was remodeled just before 1895 with stalls for six horses, while the hayloft and the gallery were much older and were put back into place above the new floor in 1895. In the outer courtyard, the old **barn**, with its brown log walls, stands along the upper side. On the lower parallel side is the former cowshed, with room for 23 cows. A continuation of the cowshed is a hayshed. Near the hayshed was a building for smaller animals, such as sheep, goats and possibly pigs. In addition, there were three more outbuildings which belonged to the previous farmer, retired and still living on the farm. There was also a **smithy**, which still stands outside the courtyards because of the risk of fire.

The old one-room schoolhouse, now divided into guestrooms, was built in the 1860's and was in use as a school until the 1920's. By the time of the fire insurance assessment of 1895, the **upper lodging house** east of the storehouses was in place. This older two-story log building was moved from the Sygard Kvamme farm in Lom, furnished with 10 guest bedrooms and equipped with a veranda in a provincial variation of the "Swiss style." The veranda is now enclosed and has six small windows, more in line with the building traditions of the area. On the

hill over the courtyard are a couple of smaller older houses with more bedrooms and a small chapel.

Norwegian country storehouses or loft buildings traditionally had guest bedrooms on the upper floors, as was the case at Røisheim. Several such rooms have become guestrooms. Around 1970, modernization was begun, and baths were installed in the rooms. This was done in close association with the National Office of Historic Monuments, and these new installations were adapted to suit the valuable cultural framework of the complex. The entire group of buildings was declared a historic monument in 1923, in the first list of protected monuments in Norway.

The hotel's large collection of antiques includes old cupboards and chests with carvings and rosepainting. A special feature of the folk art of Gudbrandsdal is its rich acanthus leaf decoration. The acanthus plant grows along the Mediterranean and formed the basis for the tendril decor of the Romans 2000 years ago. At the end of the 17th century, this type of ornament was brought to Norway by Dutch craftsmen, who used it in the new furnishings for Oslo Cathedral. From there, this type of decoration spread throughout the country during the 18th century. It became particularly popular in Gudbrandsdal and developed in forms which suited the folk art of the region. There is still a rich tradition of this type of carving in the valley.

WALAKER HOTEL
Solvorn

From generation to generation for over 300 years

During the middle of the 19th century, the tiny but beautiful village of Solvorn in Sogn could almost be considered a small harbor city. Rich Hafslo farmers shipped their products from here. Trade blossomed, and at one time, there were six or seven merchants in this little place. At that time, Solvorn also was the site of a court of law. The court sessions were held four times a year in the courtroom at Walaker Hotel. At the time, the hotel, which had guesthouse status, was the center of activity in the area.

But times changed. Roads soon connected the villages around Lustrafjord, an arm of the Sognefjord, and goods were transferred from boat to truck, so the need for a steamship office at Solvorn eventually disappeared. Today, the area is quiet and peaceful. The

beautiful old wooden houses rise in terraces from the shore and the weather-beaten boathouses cast long shadows against the mirror of the fjord. Now, Solvorn looks like a sleepy little town in the south of Norway.

The old stone table in the garden is set for lunch, with dried and cured meats and flatbread, as befits a traditional west country hotel (right).

A bridal party at Solvorn? No, just Oddlaug and Hermod Nitter Walaker boating on the fjord with their two daughters.

It's quiet by the quay. The only ship at the dock is the M/S Urnes, which carries tourists across the fjord to Urnes stave church, built in the 12th century and the oldest extant stave church in the country.

The Nitter family at Walaker

Walaker Hotel, the guesthouse by the quay, is over 300 years old and has been in the same family the entire time, passing from generation to generation. The Nitter family probably originated in Scotland. One of its members came to Bergen in the 16th century and became a businessman in western Norway. At the beginning of the 17th century, part of the family moved to Sogn. Christen Nitter, who later founded what today is Walaker Hotel, grew up in inner Sogn. Meanwhile, he left the area to learn a trade and was apprenticed to a goldsmith for several years, but in 1690, he returned to Solvorn and rented the general store at Vollåker. Together with his wife Birgitte, he began doing business in Sol-

The old sitting room, filled with antiques and older landscape paintings collected by several generations, was incorporated into the new hotel building in 1934 (above and previous pages).

Breakfast outside under the flowering apple tree. The garden in front of the hotel is an important part of the milieu.

vorn, and they earned enough to buy the store in 1696. At the same time, Christen bought Vollåker farm, and eventually many other farms. Christen and Birgitte had seven children, but it was the youngest son, Ludvig, born in 1709, who took over as trades-man and innkeeper after the father. He received his Royal license as tradesman and innkeeper on June 11, 1734. In 1758, the license was renewed and it was then noted that "Ludvig Nitter must still maintain a guesthouse and inn at Vallaker, and supply travelers and others with proper lodging, as well as food and drink as

needed and for a reasonable fee, on the condition that he brew beer for the inn on the premises, but he is not allowed to distill liquor." So Ludvig brewed beer. It was brewed with barley in the winter, so it had to be stored in a cold cellar in order to keep through the summer. For banquets and holidays, a stronger beer, with a higher alcohol content, was brewed.

New generations

Ludvig was married to Øllegård Klingenberg. When he died in 1776, his widow continued running the inn using his license, as widows were permitted to do. The pair had six children, but in 1790, the youngest son, Henrik, received the deed to the property. He was married to Mette Råum and lived at Sogndal. When Henrik applied for permission to run the inn in 1799, the county administrator wrote: "I recommend that the present owner of this place, Henrik Nitter, receive the privilege given to his father, Ludvig Nitter, in the same place in 1758. True, he owns Årøy farm in Sogndal, and as long as he lives on this farm, someone else has to run the inn at Solvorn, but those who have the right to take over Årøy might be able to buy him out, since he has to settle at Solvorn. The highest fee which can be paid yearly is 2 riksdaler." So Henrik moved back to Vollåker in 1808.

Henrik and Mette had eight children. In 1821, their son Erik, born in 1795, took over Vollåker. That same year, he applied for an innkeeper's license, and the county administrator wrote to the department that it was absolutely necessary to have a guesthouse and inn at Solvorn. The application was approved, and in 1831, he also received a storekeeper's license. In 1824, Erik married Malene Mo from Hafslo. They had a son who died young and four daughters. The eldest daughter, Mette Malene, born in 1828, received the deed to the property when her father was on his death bed. In 1845, she married Jakob Sjursen Talle, and they ran the guesthouse together. At that time, the first tourists began to come to the west country and in 1856, the Swedish-Norwegian Crown Prince, later Carl XV, traveled through Norway. He traveled over Sognefjell and out Sognefjord. Photographer Mathias Hansen accompanied him and probably took the first pictures of Solvorn and Walaker Guesthouse.

Mette Malene Nitter died in childbirth in 1868, 40 years old. It was the 11th birth in her 23-year marriage. Four of the 11 children died young, and of those who grew to adulthood, Erik, the

Walaker has its own bridal crown which has been handed down from generation to generation.

eldest son, born in 1848, took over after his father in 1878. That same year, he married Barbra Wilkensdotter Hereid from Årdal. They had six children, and their son Wilken, born in 1881, was the next generation of Nitter to take over the old family hotel.

Wilken married Inga Ragnhild Mo from Luster, who eventually became a legend as the hostess at Solvorn. She received her education at the State School of Home Economics at Stabekk (near Oslo) and had extensive work experience in large-scale catering, both from the tuberculosis sanitarium at Luster and from Helgheim County College in Sogndal. Both Inga and Wilken were also local politicians. Inga was the first woman member of the Hafslo District Council. In addition, they ran both the shipping office and the post office at Solvorn. They also laid the groundwork for a more modern hotel at Walaker in the middle of the 1930's, when they remodeled the old guesthouse to make it more functional.

Walaker Hotel today

Times have changed, generations too, but little or nothing has changed at Walaker Hotel. The old courthouse now holds a meeting room and a few guest bedrooms. A few meters away is the wooden main building, painted yellow and remodeled by Inga and Wilken in 1934. It is surrounded by a lovely, lush garden with hedges and white picket fencing. Virginia creeper climbs up the walls, and lilacs and fruit trees are in full blossom in the garden. It's no wonder that many guests enjoy breakfast outdoors. Actress Sonja Wigert, a frequent guest at Walaker, always asked for her breakfast to be served on the old stone table under the apple tree.

Just below the hotel is a lovely little sandy beach, which is very popular with summer guests. On sunny days, there are bathers everywhere.

The comfortable atmosphere at Walaker Hotel greets everyone who walks through he door. This small family-run place is more like a private home than a hotel. The host and hostess, Oddlaug and Hermod Nitter Walaker, are the eighth generation of the Nitter family at Walaker Hotel. Hermod was born and brought up at Solvorn, while Oddlaug is from Numedal. They assumed ownership in 1978, but they had managed the place along with Hermod's mother, Inga, since they married in 1968. Both are determined to continue the old traditions, and they have found a good way to divide the work. Oddlaug takes care of reservations and the practical side of the daily business, while Hermod is in charge of the kitchen. For the most part, he serves traditional Norwegian dishes. That's what the guests want, and that makes Hermod happy. And that's the most appropriate food to serve at an old, venerable hotel far up a fjord.

Until 1978, Walaker was both a farm and a hotel with the same owners. Today, it is partitioned, and while Hermod runs the hotel, his brother Erik has taken over the farm. The old barn behind the hotel, which dates from 1882, is now "Galleri Walaker 300," an art gallery, restored by Hermod and opened in May, 1990, for the hotel's 300-year jubilee.

Parts of Walaker Hotel are among the oldest in the country. The old courthouse, where people slept in two large rooms, still stands. There was one room for men and a smaller one for women. The age of the building is unknown, but it has the usual west country construction with roots in Bergen architecture from the 17th century to the beginning of the 19th century. Typical features are the simple, rectangular layout and the noticeable curve of the roof which extends only slightly over the walls. In the classic west country manner, the outer panels are placed horizontally and the windows are arranged symmetrically on the gable wall. In the 1880's, the large sleeping quarters were divided into smaller rooms.

The veranda on the long wall facing the newer hotel building probably was constructed at this time.

Two smaller farmhouses, each 1 1/2 stories over a high cellar and with gable walls facing the fjord, used

This turn-of-the-century picture shows that during the 1800's, Solvorn had grown into a town, complete with a steamship pier. In the cluster of houses in the middle of the picture are the three buildings of the guesthouse with their rows of gables facing the fjord. In front is a garden with a buttressing wall. The house at the back is Tingstova, the two-story courthouse, which is still standing. The other two houses were decisive in planning the new hotel building in 1934. Photograph: Private collection.

A small west country manor

to be alongside the courthouse. In 1934, these houses were converted into a new hotel building, and only an old lounge at the front nearest the courthouse was retained. The structure of the old buildings, however, determined that of the new one, which has two gables toward the fjord. These are connected by another building with a veranda which features pairs of classic columns in the front. The result was a very harmonious building reminiscent of a small west country manor in the Neo-Classical style from around 1800.

Bergen architect Johan Lindstrøm (1893-1958) designed the addition. He had grown up at old Hotel Lindstrøm in Lærdal. He was educated in Stockholm during a period in which it was felt that old, local building traditions from the 18th and early 19th centuries should be the determining factors for new architecture. This is evident in the buildings he later designed. Traditional shapes from Bergen and western Norway provided the departure point for a new and rational architecture. The main building at Walaker Hotel and a great number of other buildings from his hand are living expressions of his views.

Completely different ideas contributed to the building of the more modern large bungalow-style motel behind the hotel in 1964.

Even the old barn at Walaker has a history worth mentioning. It was built in 1882 with a cowshed, stable and hayloft. Cows were kept here until the 1960's, later only sheep. The building was in poor condition at its 100th birthday at the beginning of the 1980's. But, it was worth preserving, because it had been built of materials from the old 17th century church at Solvorn, which had been torn down in 1882. Inside, the log walls bear traces of its former use. Parts of the ceiling still include a border beautifully decorated with painted tendrils furling out over the surface in a manner typical of the end of the 1600's. Today, it seems brutal that old, elaborate churches were torn down and by chance, the materials end up in a barn, but this, unfortunately, was quite common in the 19th century. In order to raise money for new churches, building materials from old ones were sold at auction to whoever could use them. After the barn at Walaker was restored, it was made into an art gallery which opened in 1990. The hotel

itself also has some of the old church fixtures with different kinds of carving from the 1600's.

Urnes stave church, built in the 12th century, is on the other side of the fjord. The oldest preserved stave church in Norway, it is of the greatest art historical interest. The church is decorated with unusually many carvings featuring tendrils, dragons and other fantastic animals. In addition, many carved sections from an even older church from the 11th century have been used. These pieces are treasures of European art and have given the name to the "Urnes style" – a special type of animal ornamentation which was widespread in northwest Europe at this time. The church contains many examples of this older style of artistic decoration, with its unusually deep relief, unique from an art historical point of view. In the north wall of the church are parts of an earlier portal and a cornerpost with some of the best carvings.

HOTEL MUNDAL
Fjærland

With the Jostedal Glacier as the nearest neighbor

At the heart of the Fjærlandfjord, one of the many arms of the Sognefjord, lies the fertile agricultural settlement of Fjærland. With the Jostedal Glacier as the nearest neighbor, it was considered a perfect and idyllic place for tourism from early days. For many years, the 800-square-kilometer glacier has been one of Norway's most important tourist attractions. Two arms of the glacier, Suphelle and Bøya, stretch all the way down to Fjærland and make an ideal starting point for glacier exploration.

At the same time as the glaciers attracted the first tourists to Fjærland, they also provided work for the local inhabitants. In addition to farming and other jobs, most inhabitants also earned money as glacier guides. Mikkel Mundal was one of the settlement's most experienced guides. He was born in 1857, and with his sister Brita, he ran the general store and guesthouse at Fjærland quay. They started out small, and the general store and guesthouse were in the same building. During the winter, Mikkel managed the business alone, but during the summer, Brita and her husband, Olaus Dahle, came from Lærdal to help. Olaus was born in 1847 in Isfjorden in Romsdal and came to Vangsnes in Sogn as a teacher and choir singer. In Vangsnes, he met Brita Mundal. They married in 1888 and moved to Lærdal where Olaus continued his work as a teacher.

From guesthouse to hotel
Gradually, the number of visitors to Fjærland increased. Glacier explorers, artists, royal and regular tourists came to experience the glacier and the powerful landscape around Sognefjord. The guesthouse on the pier soon proved to be too small, so Brita and Olaus decided to build a proper hotel.

Together with Brita's half-brother Johannes, and her brothers Mikkel and Per, they started building, and on June 29th, 1891, they opened Hotel Mundal. This handsome building had taken only a year to build. With its intricate detail and its characteristic round tower, this wooden castle in Fjærland had become one of

Hotel Mundal is run by sisters-in-law Marit Orheim Mauritzen (on the right) and Billie Orheim (on the left). Behind them is Marit's daughter Brita.

The music room provides rich opportunity for musical breaks and has a wonderful view of the fjord, mountains, and glaciers. The ceiling in the tower bay window, framed with darkened wood panels and stenciled paintings, is representative of its era (right).

Sogn and Fjordane's largest buildings. But then it had cost all of 36,000 crowns to build, a fantastic sum at the time!

Numerous sources of revenue

Johannes and Olaus each owned half, but Brita and Olaus managed the hotel. In 1906, Brita and Olaus bought out Johannes and became sole owners. Olaus gave up his teaching position in Lærdal, and the family moved to Fjærland to run the hotel all year round. It wasn't always easy to make ends meet. The time during the First World War was especially difficult. Guests stayed away, and the hosts had to find other means of survival. That's when Brita's weaving activities came in handy. She was a master behind the loom and was soon known for her beautiful woven work far beyond Fjærland's borders. Most of what she made was sold to guests at the hotel. Some years, sales of her woven items comprised 30% of the families income. Fortunately, the family kept some of Brita's floor coverings and drapes, and these are still in use at the hotel today.

In addition, Olaus had his pension, and to add to the income, the family also had a small farm. They kept cows, pigs, and chickens up to the 1950's.

A new generation

Brita and Olaus had six children: daughters Margit, Gudrun, Sunniva, and Borghild, and sons Sigurd and Olaf.

In 1935, Sigurd, who studied engineering and worked in the Færoe Islands, came home to run the hotel. He had help from his siblings, especially from Marit and Olaf, who both lived in Fjærland. The tourist trade increased steadily during the 1930's, and eventually, extra rooms were needed. Sigurd raised the roof in the attic for extra bedrooms, and he added hot and cold running water to all the rooms. The work was done carefully, so as not to ruin the character of the hotel. Unfortunately, he did not insulate the building, so the water had to be turned off each autumn, so that frost would not burst the pipes. Because of this, Hotel Mundal has remained closed during the winter. But the tourist traffic continued to increase, and in 1939 Sigurd again had to expand. This time, he extend the dining room and added ten more beds upstairs.

Then came the Second World War. Again, visitors stopped coming, so there was nothing to do but close the hotel for five years. After the war, guests returned, and these years were dominated mostly by English tourists visiting Fjærland.

The round corner tower encircled by balconies is the architectural high point of this grand building.

A family-run hotel

Sigurd died suddenly in 1957 and Borghild took over the hotel. She had a university degree in physics and was married to Odd Orheim from Bærum. She was the only one of the six siblings to marry. Borghild was a lecturer in Bergen until 1971, so in reality, her siblings ran the hotel, except during school holidays. Margit and Olaf continued to live in Fjærland, and Sunniva and Gudrun moved back in 1957 and 1958 respectively. Gudrun, who was trained as a teacher, looked after the guest correspondence. Sunniva wove new floor coverings and sewed. Margit, a trained chef, was responsible for the kitchen. Gudrun and Sunniva both loved gardening, and they deserve the credit for the beautiful garden that surrounds Hotel Mundal today.

Borghild was responsible for the next large addition to the hotel, when she added bathrooms to all the rooms in the north wing. It was necessary to move the northern wall out a bit to avoid reducing the number of guest beds. This did, however, cause a slight breach of style, but it was necessary to maintain the hotel's capacity, so it could receive the tour groups which were the basis the hotel's business in the 60's and 70's.

Borghild Orheim helped American vice-president Walter Mondale trace his Norwegian roots, and there were great festivities when he visited Hotel Mundal in 1979.

The fireplace room was decorated in the 1920's. Artist Eiler Prytz decorated the walls, and the beautiful leather furniture made in Fjærland is still in use.

The music room has retained its original style and is one of the hotel's most popular sitting rooms. The family at Mundal has always been musical, and singing and playing music are a regular part of daily life at this traditional hotel.

Hotel Mundal Today

Borghild Orheim died in 1982. Her husband Odd had died four years earlier. They had three children, Olav, Marit, and Alv. Their daughter, Marit Orheim Mauritzen, took over the hotel after her mother died. She has a business degree and lives in Stavanger. She and her husband, Sverre Mauritzen, continued to run the hotel during their holidays as a hobby until 1986. Until then, the only way to reach Fjærland was by ferry up the fjord. Then a new road with a tunnel under the Jostedal Glacier to Skei in Jølster was opened. This created a new type of business, and Marit quit her job as office manager at Rogaland College in Stavanger and became a full time hotelier. Hotel Mundal is a large and expensive hotel, both to maintain and to run, so there is more than enough to do. But she, too, has help from her family, especially from her sister-in-law Billie. Billie is English, a trained orthopedist, and is married to Marit's brother Olav. They live in Røyken, but every summer, Billie leaves Østlandet to run the hotel with Marit. The have gradually raised the standard of the hotel, and today, all rooms have baths and telephones.

In 1991, Queen Sonja opened the Glacier Museum in Fjærland, and in 1994, the community got a new road connection, this time to Sogndal. In the summer of 1996, the "Norwegian book town" was established in Fjærland, so now the settlement is a paradise for book lovers, with many used book stores, specialty old book stores, and book cafes. And, with easier access and new tourist attractions, the old family hotel by the glacier has entered a new, and well-deserved renaissance.

It took only one year to build Hotel Mundal in 1890-1891. It was designed by Peter Andreas Blix, the architect responsible for Fleischer's Hotel at Voss. Hotel Mundal is in the Gothic Revival style, as is Fleischer's, with a steep roof and dormers with pointed gables. The combination of different shapes is, however, completely different. Both hotels are distinctive, and no others can be compared with them elsewhere in Norway.

A special feature at Hotel Mundal is the powerful corner tower surrounded by a veranda on both floors and crowned with a cone-shaped roof. It is said that the builders demanded such a tower from the architect. It gives the building a similar type of medieval castle effect as at Fleischer's Hotel.

Steep roofs, the tower, and pointed gables were inspired by medieval castles in this hotel from the end of the 1800's.
Photograph from the 1890's.

Castle tower and patina

The rather fantastic construction has been reduced somewhat over the years. Two pointed gables on the north wall have been removed, and the steep roofs have been lifted in places to add space for proper windows in new attic rooms. This was done in the late 1930's, when functionalism was in style. Very little attention was paid to the romantic architecture of earlier periods, which had its roots in even earlier times. Considering the conditions, the alteration of the roofs at Mundal is restrained.

Many lounges from the earliest days of the hotel are still intact. They have dark oiled ceilings, in which beams and panels are arranged in a pattern and are partly decorated with stencils. In the corner salon, the tower forms a bay with a wonderful view of the fjord toward the glaciers. In the 1920's, artist Eiler Prytz

painted garlands of flowers on the walls of the fireplace room. The leather easy chairs from that time are still in use. In the 1930's, the dining room was enlarged and the walls were wainscoted. Upstairs, more guestrooms were added.

Here, too, sanitary and technical conditions have been improved. Toilets were installed in 1907, the first bathrooms in 1923. In 1915, electricity was installed for both light and heating. Hot and cold water was installed in all rooms in the 1930's, and private baths in the 1960's and 1970's. The hotel never needed an ice house, for the glaciers were practically outside the door, but an electric freezer was installed in the cellar in 1949.

Even with all the technical improvements, Hotel

Mundal is not a completely modern hotel. It is comfortable, but the original installations and old furnishings are still much in evidence, and they glow with the patina of long use. This is part of the ambiance at the traditional, family-run hotel. The hotel features many woven tapestries on the walls and on the floor, brought to the hotel by hostess Brita Dahle. Some were woven from designs by well-known artists, while others are in the traditional checkerboard pattern which has been typical of the area for centuries.

The glaciers have always been among the hotel's greatest attractions. In 1991, the Norwegian Glacier Museum was opened just a few kilometers away. Both the exhibitions and the museum building itself are worth a visit. Designed by the internationally honored Norwegian architect, Sverre Fehn, the building is constructed in concrete, wood and glass, its shape derived from the glaciers themselves. It has become the destination of many architects in what used to be isolated and remote countryside.

KVIKNE'S HOTEL – BALHOLM
Balestrand

The fairy tale castle on the Sognefjord

Kvikne's Hotel has always been considered the most fashionable of the many beautiful wooden hotels in the region of Sogn og Fjordane. This proud landmark rises over the terrain and reminds us of bygone days, when artists and tourists flocked to Balestrand at the turn of the century.

That was when the first "floating hotels," ships of a size never seen before in western Norway, docked outside Balestrand, and the passengers went on land and promenaded along the streets of the tiny town.

In those days, rich Norwegian and foreign tourists built elegant summer houses in the "Swiss style" along the beach at Balestrand and came sailing in to the hotel on their own private yachts.

That was when men in light summer suits played croquet on the grounds of the hotel, while ladies in long white dresses, straw hats and parasols strolled along the beach. Every evening, there were grand garden parties, where everyone danced the summer night away.

The most famous artists in the land, such as Hans Dahl and Adelsten Normann, came to paint the impressive landscapes of western Norway, and kings and kaisers, such as King Haakon, Kaiser Wilhelm of Germany, Queen Wilhelmina of the Netherlands and the Prince of Egypt, came to admire them.

Then, as now, Kvikne's Hotel was there – a modern-day castle and the natural gathering place.

Kvigne in Lærdal in Sogn. One stayed home to run the farm, while the other two went off to see the world. Knut went to America to seek his fortune, and Ole went to Balestrand, or Balholm as it was called at the time, and became a clerk at a general store there.

The store was called Holmen and had been established in 1752 by Nicolai Gierløw from Bergen. Since then, it had changed owners many times. When Ole arrived at Balholm, Johannes Danielsen, also from Bergen, owned and ran the place. In Danielsen's operating license from 1863, it mentions that he also was obligated to "receive travelers and offer them food and lodging." Danielsen was an innkeeper as well as a merchant.

When Ole started working for Danielsen at Holmen, he was only 18 years old, an outgoing and lively lad. He enjoyed his work from the beginning, and he and Danielsen got along just fine. Ole was industrious and hard-working, and not too many years had passed before he had saved enough money to buy his own place. He noticed that more and more English tourists were coming to Balestrand and realized that there was money to be made. Now he wanted to work for himself!

When Danielsen heard of Ole's plans, he offered him Holmen instead. By then, Danielsen was an old man. He had never married, so he had no heirs. So on February 26, 1877, Ole Kvigne signed a contract with Johannes Danielsen and took over both the store and the inn with room for four guests.

"A room with a view." There are many of them at Kvikne's Hotel! The veranda's construction is typical of its time and is just as beautiful from the inside as from the outside (right).

With its long verandas looking out over Sognefjord, Kvikne's is the largest and most impressive of our wooden hotels (next pages).

The story begins
Castle or no castle. There would not have been a story at all, had there not been three brothers from the tiny mountain farm of

The letter from America

Two years earlier, Ole had married Kari Gurvin from Sogndal. Now he had both a wife and an inn. He was ready to receive the influx of tourists he had waited for and dreamed about ever since he saw the first steamship on the Sognefjord in the 1850's. The only thing which worried him was that the inn had only four beds.

But one day, Ole received a letter from his brother Knut, five years his elder, who had emigrated. Knut had done well "over there" and had saved some money which he wanted to invest in his brother's business. Did his brother want him, too?

Ole did indeed, and Knut returned from America, not only with a bulging wallet, but also with a new name. The Americans could not pronounce Kvigne, so he had changed it to Kvikne. Ole thought immediately of all the foreign tourists coming to Bale-

strand, and then he, too, changed his name. From then on, both brothers used the name Kvikne.

Although brothers, Ole and Knut were not at all alike. The Englishman, F. Scarlett, one of the pioneers of Norwegian travel, described them in his book, "Norway as a Tourist Country": Ole was plump, ruddy and clean-shaven, while Knut was dark as a southern European, with coal-black hair and a large mustache. And according to Scarlett, Ole was still outgoing and jolly, while Knut was quiet and introverted.

But the two brothers worked well together. Ole and Kari took care of daily operations and dealt with the guests, while Knut maintained the buildings and organized leisure activities for the guests. He knew the mountains around Balestrand, and after years in America, he spoke excellent English. He became a popular guide, in fact, so popular that he married one of the

But all the work had sapped Ole's strength, and the same year the hotel was finished, he died of a heart attack, only 64 years old, in September, 1913. A few months later, the First World War began, and just before Christmas that same year, on December 18, 1914, Knut also died.

Ole's son, Theodor, who had attended hotel and catering college abroad, took over Kvikne's Hotel. When Balestrand Electric Company was established that same year, he had electric lights installed at the hotel. But tragedy struck the Kvikne family again, and in 1916, Theodor died, only 34 years old. His mother, Kari, died the following year.

Theodor's brother, Sigurd, took over the hotel. He, too, had a thorough hotel and catering education, and he had trained at Kvikne's. He and his wife Marta ran the hotel according to the

The impressive Høyvik room has an unique collection of dragon-style furniture made by the Balestrand carver Ivar Høyvik between 1910-1959.

A detail from the Høyvik room showing the high quality of Ivar Høyvik's carving (belowe).

guests in the middle of the 1880's, Margaret Green, daughter of an English vicar.

Always expanding
During the first years that Ole and Knut ran the inn, the ferry stopped at Balestrand only once a week. But as Balestrand became more and more popular, both with Norwegian and foreign tourists, the ferries stopped more often.

Soon, they needed more than four beds, and so the brothers began adding on to the guesthouse. The last expansion was begun in 1912, and the following year, the large wooden hotel building was finished, and it still stands today. 36 years after Ole bought the inn at Balholm, it had become Norway's largest fjord hotel, with 200 beds.

Every room in the house is rich in detail. There is a collection of pictures of royal guests who have visited Kvikne's over the years.

The hotel has a large collection of landscape paintings from the area around Sognefjord. They represent the different eras' artistic interpretations of this lovely area.

traditions established by Ole and Knut. Good year's followed. Tourism blossomed and Balestrand was a popular destination. In addition to Scandinavians, Englishmen and Germans, more and more tourists came from the United States. The Norwegian American Line was established in 1912, and after the First World War, ships sailed directly from the US to Norway. Many Norwegian-Americans used this opportunity to see the old country once again.

Marta Kvikne - a legend

In the fall of 1935, another tragedy struck. Sigurd died unexpectedly, and Marta was left with four children and one of Norway's largest hotels. But the years she had run the hotel with Sigurd had given her valuable experience and indispensable insight in running a business, as well as knowledge of human nature. Kvikne's Hotel had an excellent reputation, both at home and abroad, but Marta realized that in order to keep that reputation, the hotel had

to be modernized. In 1937, she began to install hot and cold water in the guest bedrooms, as well as showers and toilets in the corridors. The following year, the dining room received a much-needed facelift.

Soon Marta at Kvikne's became a legend, as her mother-in-law Kari had been before her. Through the difficult years during World War II and the tough times following the war, Marta held on. During the summer of 1940, she closed the hotel, but she kept it open during the rest of the war. This was wonderful for those Norwegians who could escape the cities and the worries of the war and enjoy a vacation in quiet surroundings.

During the first years of peace, she had to deal with food shortages, ration cards and price restraints. But Marta never gave up, and under her firm, but mild and generous leadership, Kvikne's Hotel remained popular with both Norwegian and foreign tourists.

New times – new standards

As time went by, Marta and Sigurd's son, Per, began working at the hotel, and in 1961, Marta entrusted the family hotel to him and his wife Mulla. During the last few years, the hotel seemed too small. There were enough lounges, but there just weren't enough guest bedrooms with baths. Per decided to expand, and after three different stages of building, a new and modern annex was finished in 1973. A new wing behind the old wooden hotel housed 165 new and much-needed rooms.

Sigurd Kvikne, son of Per and Mulla, and the fourth generation of Kviknes at the hotel, took over after his father died in 1991. Since then, he has remodeled all the rooms in the older part of the hotel. Each of the 50 rooms has been refurbished in the old style, so that today, guests can once again experience the hotel as it was when new in 1913.

And the fairy tale continues as it began, to the delight of new generations of Norwegians, Germans, Americans, Englishmen, Japanese, Swedes and Italians, who continue to visit the white fairy tale castle by the Sognefjord.

The large fantastic wooden building at Kvikne's Hotel is evidence of the tremendous growth in tourism at Balestrand from the middle of the 1880's until the First World War. During the 1880's, numerous annexes were built onto the old guesthouse and the original general store which had been built in traditional west country style. In 1890, there was a more extensive renovation to make a unified building with three verandas at the front and a tower with roof terrace in the middle. But that was not enough, and in 1894, a completely new, large building was opened. This building is the eastern-most third of the hotel today. In 1912, the old building from 1890 was demolished, and the newest

filled with fantastic gingerbread carving that they look like fine lace. Between the dormers, the long rows of verandas are broken rhythmically for variation. Neither before nor after has there been such lavish treatment of verandas in Norway.

Modernization is also part of the hotel's history. In the 1930's, hot and cold water was installed in the rooms, and at the end of the decade, the dining room was extended for the first time. In 1959, a sprinkler system was installed to protect the building in case of fire, the first of its kind in a Norwegian tourist hotel. In the 1960's, the modern concrete building was erected behind the wooden one without any attempt to adapt it to the old building. Not only was the

On the main floor, the dining room and large lounges face the fjord. They retain their original brown oiled beamed ceiling with panels and painted stenciled designs. Landscape paintings from the region decorate the walls. The hotel has an impressive collection of furniture with dragon style carving inspired by medieval Norwegian stave churches and their portals. This furniture dates from the time around 1900, and most pieces have been at the hotel from the beginning.

The dragon style also appears in architecture many places near the hotel, where both Norwegians and foreigners built richly decorated summer houses from about 1890 to the beginning of World War I.

An elaborate veranda facade in a grand format

building from 1894 extended to the west by almost 2/3, in the same style. Completed in 1913, that resulted in the grand, symmetrical facade facing the fjord, which still stands today.

With its enormous dimensions and unusually rich decoration with gables and verandas on the entire fjord facade, this wooden building, dating from 1894-1913, is a unique example of the so-called "Swiss style" in Norwegian wooden architecture. Originally, it was even more decorative, with a row of verandas also in front of the entire cellar floor. On the roofs between the large dormers, where the roof has been raised to make room for larger windows on the attic floor, there were once 21 small dormers with pointed gables. This made the facade even more lively than it is today. In spite of the changes, it is still an impressive building, concrete evidence of the importance of tourism at the turn of the century. The protruding wings on the sides and the larger dormers with pointed gables give the facade a harmonious rhythm, with emphasis on the middle and outer wings, where the gabled verandas have different shapes and the beam constructions are so

wooden building regarded as old-fashioned, it also was considered ugly and repulsive by both guests and owners. At one time, it was in danger of demolition. Now, that view has changed completely, and the old wooden hotel is more popular than ever. The old rooms have been renovated and equipped with private baths so that today's guests can enjoy the comfort they demand. Some rooms have been combined to make small suites.

In 1890, the old guesthouse was expanded in different stages to become a large hotel with three verandas and a square central tower with a roof terrace (on the left). Four years later, a large new annex was built (on the right). In 1913, it was extended to become the large wooden hotel of today. Photograph: Knud Knudsen, about 1894, Bergen University Library.

Most of these houses are still painted in the original strong red color with white and green trim as was typical at Balestrand. A church inspired by stave churches was built for English tourists at the beginning of this century. These buildings are picturesque dots on the magnificent landscape, well worthy of a promenade.

HUSUM HOTELL
Borgund

A salmon paradise on the Lærdal River

For many hundreds of years, ever since the Middle Ages, the most important land connection between eastern and western Norway has been through Lærdal. On foot, on horseback, with horse and carriage, and later by car, people have journeyed through this steep, narrow valley where European Route 16 today winds its way between steep mountainsides along the Lærdal River down in the bottom of the valley. Husum Hotel, one of the best preserved

The guests at Husum are primarily salmon fishermen. There is an old rack by the door for hanging fishing caps and walking sticks.

wooden hotels in Sogn, is right by the road. Next to nothing has been changed since the last great expansion in 1887. The white buildings have retained their beautiful verandas and fantastic projections with carvings to rival the finest lace. Mighty mountains rise just behind the hotel, and just below it flows Norway's most famous salmon river. From June to August each year, "the Queen of Rivers," as it is called locally, is an eldorado for salmon fishermen from around the world. This period is still the busiest at Husum Hotel, as it has been for more than 100 years.

But Husum is not just for nature lovers and sports fishermen. Vindhellavegen, the old royal road through Borgund and Lærdal, goes right by the hotel, and only three kilometers away is Borgund stave church, built around 1150, one of the most beautiful and best preserved in the country. And 25 kilometers from Husum, right on the Sognefjord, is Lærdalsøyri, with its picturesque old wooden houses.

From farm to inn
There has been a farm at Husum since the Middle Ages. Husum is the old written plural for house, and therefore, it is likely that the small collection of buildings on the site originally gave the farm its name.

The basis for running a hotel at Husum farm was a 1648 law, which stipulated that there should be an inn every 10 kilometers on the main road. Every 30 kilometers "a rich and handsome man on a good, convenient farm" was designated as an innkeeper. In 1834, Halvor Husum applied for an inn on the farm. In connection with that, he received a reference from Parson Bull, dated August 17, 1834, in which the parson notes that there can be no doubt

The salon has new wood-paneled walls and furniture from the end of the 19th century in a stylistic blend of Renaissance Revival and Pseudo-Rococo (right).

regarding the "appropriateness" of an inn at Husum. He recommended that Halvor receive the license. He also mentioned casual references from travelers who had enjoyed Halvor's hospitality. Really, the pastor's letter gives the impression that the inn at Husum was already developing of its own accord.

The next year, all the formalities were in order, and 1835 is considered the first year for the hotel and inn at Husum. A separate hotel building was constructed, and from 1850, Husum was a "permanent inn."

Before the Oslo-Bergen Railroad opened in 1909, almost all mail was sent from eastern to western Norway via Lærdal. Postal transport was, of course, on horseback, and eventually also this form of transport was associated more and more with coaching inns, where trustworthy farmers were given responsibility for the mail. They were not paid for this, but they enjoyed certain privileges, such as exemption from military service. Husum was a postal station from 1858. When the mail arrived from the nearest station, horses always had to be ready to carry the post to the next station. It was always exciting when the mail came from Bergen on its way to Christiania. In around 1860, with the addition of the telegraph, a separate building was constructed to house the post and telegraph office.

Salmon fishermen

There were many busy days at Husum. In 1860, Halvor's son Roar and his wife Sigrid took over the hotel and ran it until 1900, when their son, Ole, took over. Both Roar and Ole were popular innkeepers. Tourism in western Norway was growing, and in the years around the turn of the century, the number of tourists at Husum Hotel increased steadily.

A travel guide from 1893 gives the following description: "Husum - excellent. Large new building, expanded in 1887. Large dining hall; 23 rooms, including 18 bedrooms with 30 beds. Toilet for travelers. Ice house. Good fishing of trout and salmon."

Borgund stave church, built in the 1100's, is one of Norway's best preserved stave churches, with exceptionally rich decoration.

At Husum, there was an ice house, where the fishermen could store their catches. Enthusiastic sports fishermen returned year after year. There were especially many regular visitors from England. It is said that every year, a telegram was sent to London as soon as the first salmon had "passed Sæltun Bridge."

Famous people of the day

But it was not just salmon fishermen who came to Husum. Others came to experience the valley's imposing and contrast-filled scenery. From flat Lærdalsøyri, the valley narrows down to the point where there's only room for the river and the road. Hans Konow descriptively characterized it in this way in 1845: "Enormous blocks of rock which have fallen from the mountain, and which, along with other blocks, frame and hang over the road. It takes courage to pass through. The eye meets the overhanging stones that seem in the midst of falling. They defy the law of gravity and forever hang as an amazing threat and terror to travelers." Of course, the roads have been improved, and the trip from Lærdalsøyri to Husum Hotel takes less than an hour. Back then, it took an entire day.

Eventually, the valley became famous, and all the famous men of the day came to the hotel, starting with King Oscar II. The old guestbooks list such names as authors Bjørnstjerne Bjørnson and Emile Zola, painter Gerhard Munthe, and composers Edvard Grieg and Ole Bull.

Husum's verandas are not just beautiful in their own right. They are practical, too, providing a fantastic view of the Lærdal river, Norway's most famous salmon fishing river.

Old traditions and homemade food

Ever since it opened in 1835, Husum Hotel has been run by the same family. In 1934, Roar Husum took over the hotel and ran it until 1980, when Knut and Ingeborg Husum took it over.

Today, Knut and Ingeborg's daughter Ranveig and her husband, Ove Heggenes, run Husum. They are the sixth generation and administer both the hotel and the farm, with help of Ranveig's mother. They run the hotel much as their predecessors did. The many regular guests insure that the place stays much the same. And the food, too, is traditional. The fish dinners at Husum are famous, and bread and cakes are always homemade. It's a lot of work, but that's the order of the day at Husum. Guarding the traditions at a cultural treasure is a big responsibility, and the family know that.

At Husum, the farm buildings are still important elements in the landscape alongside the hotel building and annex. Earlier, the group of farm buildings with barns, sheds, etc. was west of the houses, but the last outbuildings were moved to a more discrete place to the east, behind the annex, in 1909-1910.

A separate hotel building was constructed at Husum quite early, perhaps in the 1830's It was a two-story unpaneled log building, and today, it

In 1871, the buildings at Husum still consisted of Lærdal's traditional log houses with turf roofs and looked more like a farm than a hotel. On the left is the oldest hotel building from the middle of the 1800's. It was expanded and altered in 1887 and is still the hotel's main building. Photograph: Knud Knudsen, Bergen University Library.

Restraint with a beautiful veranda

is the east wing of the current hotel building. The original log building had a terrace in front, with steps leading up from the farmyard, and a central entrance, where the main entrance still is today. The building was paneled and painted white towards the end of the 1870's. At the same time, a new house was built for the hosts and their staff, which today faces the road. It originally stood with unpaneled log walls for quite some time. What is now the annex was then a small, old one-floor log building, the "kårhus," where the retired former host lived. The fire insurance appraisal in 1879 described ten houses making up the yard. There were the two small storehouses, which still are a distinctive and cheerful addition to the yard, and there were both new and old stables and a grain barn, in addition to the newer haybarn. There was a cowshed, another for the sheep, and a carriage house built next to the stables.

In 1887, the hotel was expanded and equipped with its richly decorated verandas, which are still well preserved and give the building its special and amusing character. The expansion housed the dining room on the first floor and guest bedrooms on the second. The large dining room had a much higher ceiling than the rest of the building and contributes to the varied and balanced asymmetricality of the structure today. The additions were inspired by historicist wooden architecture. It is particularly evident in the large ceiling rafters which are crowned with decorated boards on the gable apexes, and on the verandas with their unusually rich gingerbread work between the elegant beam constructions and in the banisters. The same arrangement had been used the year before at Lindstrom's hotel further down the valley, and we know that the architect there was Johan Daniel Faye from Bergen. Perhaps he also designed the extension at Husum. Or maybe the builders just copied the latest style from Lindstrom's hotel. If that is true, they did a very good job!

Many ate lunch in the spacious dining room on the journey by horse and carriage between Lærdalsøyri and the large hotel up at Maristuen, which took an entire day. The dining room walls and ceiling were decorated with painted ornament which still exists today. During the expansion of the hotel in 1887, a new kitchen and pantry were added behind the old building, and an ice house was built behind the dining room. The ice was cut during the winter and stored in sawdust to keep salmon caught in the river and other foodstuffs fresh during the heat of the summer. The former kitchen in the old building was converted into a modern luxury, described as a "toilet room," presumably a washroom for dusty long distance travelers.

Around 1900, the old pensioner's building was either replaced or rebuilt with an extra floor into an annex with guest bedrooms. For a time, there were also guest bedrooms in the hosts' house. The coaching inn required a lot of stable space, for in summer months, the stable sometimes housed as many as 12 horses. The large farm contributed food for the guests and filled the many outer farm buildings until recently. Milk was produced at the farm until the 1950's.

Husum Hotel has been unusually well preserved since its renovations and additions in 1887. Modernization has been limited and the hotel has avoided major changes. Because of this, it has retained much of its original atmosphere and simplicity. The lounge includes some old furniture suites in the Pseudo-Rococo and Renaissance Revival styles. The finest elements at Husum have to be the opulent verandas which meet visitors as they enter the farmyard. The atmospheric moonlight lamps, so typical of their time, still light up the verandas at Husum.

A bit further up the valley from Husum is Borgund stave church, dating from the 1100's, the best preserved of Norway's 28 stave churches. It is also the most richly decorated and has served as a model for the restoration of other stave churches. The old road on the stretch between Husum and Borgund is another attraction. The current road, which follows the river, was built around 1870. Before then, impressive Vindhella Road, which snakes its way up the steep passes on stone walls, was the only road. It was first built around 1790, and 50 years later, the steepest parts were widened to their present state. Now, it is a popular walking path. The even older riding and pack road is also preserved, the so-called Sverrestigen, said to have been used by King Sverre in the 1100's, when he passed through the valley. This indicates that there has been heavy traffic through Lærdal since before recorded history.

HAAKONSÆT HOTEL
Hovet

In the shelter of Hallingdal

Haakonsæt Hotel lies between east and west along National Route 50 between Hol and Aurland. The exact address is Hovet, a small idyllic settlement in the beautiful Hallingdal valley countryside.

Johannes Halvorsen Teigen-Haakonsæt and his wife, Kristi Annfinset Sveinsdotter, founded both the settlement of Hovet and Haakonsæt Hotel. They bought a large piece of land in the middle of the 1800's, and Johannes started clearing the area of its original pine forest. They built a farm and started cultivating the land. In 1888, they opened Hovet's first general store. A few years later, the rural post office opened, and in 1914, a telephone exchange.

Trade blossomed, and Kristi and Johannes did well. But Johannes was often ill and became an invalid early, so Kristi looked after the business. Eventually, more shops opened in the settlement so she decided to close the general store in 1929. But Kristi was an enterprising woman, and despite much toil and trouble, she never gave up. She and her son Halvor began to make plans to build a hotel at Hovet. Kristi's brother Lars was a wealthy businessman in London, and the story is that he hired an English architect to design the new hotel.

Trials and tribulations

But life was certainly not easy for Kristi. Her husband was lame and sentenced to a life in a wheelchair. Of the three children she bore, only Halvor lived a long life. Her other son died of tuberculosis at the age of 23, and her daughter died of the same disease on Christmas Eve at the age of 32. She left behind a daughter, Alma, who was only two years old when her mother died in 1924. Because of this, Alma was raised by her grandmother Kristi, and thus she had the hotel business in her blood from an early age. English sports fisherman were frequent guests at the hotel in the years before the Second World War. They loved the English style

Alma Kaupang is the third generation of Kaupang at Haakonsæt. Today, she runs the hotel with help from her children. Both she and her son Bjørn are wearing the local Hallingdal bunad (costume).

The architectural style of Haakonsæt Hotel is more reminiscent of an urban villa than the traditional Hallingdal country style. More traditional characteristics can be seen in the old shop building from 1888, to the right in the photograph (left).

ambiance of the hotel, and Alma heard many an exiting fish story. One of their regular guests was Lord Ponsonby, who reserved the entire hotel for the summer of 1940. But the German invasion made this impossible.

Closed down and reopened

Kristi died in 1951, and Alma and her uncle Halvor inherited the hotel. They had grown up as brother and sister and were the best of friends. After the war, most of the visitors at Haakonsæt were Danish and Norwegian. The hotel was often busy, but Alma and Halvor had some good times during the years they ran the hotel together. Alma married Paul Kaupang, who had a shop and a cabin brokerage just across the street from Haakonsæt Hotel. But Alma's husband also died before his time, in 1973, at the age of only 55. Now Alma was left with the responsibility for the shop, the cabin brokerage, a farm, and four children, as well as the hotel. When Halvor died in 1986, she decided to close the hotel.

The traditional family hotel was rented out for other operations, but on July 2, 1992, it opened its doors once more to tourists and other travelers.

Nostalgia and atmosphere

Alma still owns the hotel, and she runs it together with her children. With the new year-round road between Hol and Aurland, a unique opportunity has arisen at Hovet, the possibility of year-round business. The place is a paradise for nature lovers, sport fishermen, and sportsmen. The area around Hallingskarvet can be explored all year round. In the summer, the area is perfect for walking and hiking, and in the winter, it is ideal for cross-country skiing. And, it is only a ten-minute drive to Hallingsdalskarvet Ski Center. The Hallingdal River, teeming with trout, runs directly behind the hotel. The hotel has fishing rights to the river, and guests are welcome to try their luck at any time. The same applies to idyllic Damtjern, an excellent fishing lake which lies 1100 meters above sea level, about an hour's drive from the hotel. Indeed, there are many well-stocked lakes in the area. The terrain is also very popular with hunters who come to the area to hunt roedeer, deer, moose, reindeer, hare, and ptarmigan.

This old and venerable hotel still has a reason for being. Here the important facets are atmosphere, nostalgia, well being, and tradition.

The light and airy dining room is partially furnished with the original hotel furniture.

The furnishings are a combination of old and new (far left).

In great contrast with its environment, Haakonsæt Hotel lies in a meadow at the bottom of the valley, surrounded by traditional Hallingdal style scorched log houses. The building was finished in 1933. According to family tradition, it was built

on the garden side, with entry, office, stairwell and kitchen on the courtyard side. Although the stairwell is made of relatively simple shapes, it has a monumental effect with its large fireplace in one corner and the stairs which curve elegantly up to the guest

more comfortable. In addition, there are other Pseudo-Rococo touches. Most of the guest rooms have been refurbished, and the baths in the corridors have been redone.

An upper class villa

according to drawings purchased from an English architect by a relative in London, but it is not easy to identify anything particularly English about the building as it stands today, very well preserved in its original appearance.

The house incorporates shapes which were quite common in Norwegian villa architecture during the time from around the First World War through the 1930's. The cubic shape, with a simple rectangular floor plan and the high hipped roof, which descends from a central apex down to all four walls, is typical of the time. The corners are marked with pilasters, or flat, column-like cases, and central balcony is supported by pillars with the same detailing. Only two small bay windows and the main entrance door on the side break the symmetry of the facades. The shapes express a classic grace. Neo-Classical architecture from the end of the 18th and beginning of the 19th centuries was the usual source of inspiration for buildings of this period.

Inside, the floor plan is typical for a villa of that time, with dining room and two reception rooms

bedrooms on the next floor. The white-scrubbed wooden panel also contributes to the effect. In the light dining room, some of the original Pseudo-Rococo chairs have been retained. The lounges recently were repapered in light colors, and the new furnishings are

The exterior of Haakonsæt Hotel has not been changed since it was built in 1933. Photo: Haakonsæt Hotel.

The original shop building from 1888 stands at the entrance to the driveway to the hotel. It was later used as a dwelling. It originated as a Halling cottage which eventually acquired a two-story "Swiss style" veranda facing the road and an addition at the back. The shop was shut long ago, but the building serves as a reminder of the host family's history here.

AABELHEIM GUESTHOUSE & VANGEN MOTEL
Aurland

Parsonage and captain's house in the Sogn Alps

"We sail in towards the Sogn Alps – up Aurlandfjord, which cuts between the mountains in a northeasterly direction away from mighty Sognefjord. At Beitelen, the fjord arm forks off, and Nærø-fjord continues in a westerly direction towards Gudvangen, while the other continues to the northeast to Flåm.

It is as if the mountains are throwing themselves out – steep and wild, hanging over. And the whistle from the steamboat resounds through the mountains –we are docking at Aurland.

Aurland is a large mass of mountain rock where people live only in the cracks. The better part of the area is uninhabited and undeveloped, and it never can be developed, partly because it is only rock and mountain, and partly because it lies at such high altitude that the climate is too harsh."

From Nils Lamberg's description of Aurland in Bergen's "Aften-blad" (evening paper) from July 29, 1933, one might think that this fantastic, beautiful area in western Norway is "a place where no one could imagine that anyone could live." Meanwhile, people have lived at Aurland since time immemorial, for it was once a holy cult locale where heathen gods were worshipped.

During the 17th and 18th centuries, Aurlandsvangen, center of the municipality today, was the drilling ground for the Aurland Company, part of the Northern Bergenhus Regiment, which was established to comply with Kristian IV's war ordinance of 1628. The Aurland Company's leader was Colonel Jacob Gerhard Meidell. At that time, he and Captain Mathias Juell were the most important men in the district, and they made their mark on Aurlandsvangen.

Aabelheim Guesthouse

From 1719, Colonel Meidel lived permanently at Aurland, where he had a house on Vinjum farm. But the house burned down in 1752, and he then moved to Aurlandsvangen, where he built a new house on the site of Aabelheim Guest House today. The Colonel died in 1768, but his descendants lived in the house until 1822.

At the beginning of the 1830's, the property was sold to a parson, Ole Aabel, great-grandfather and great-great-grandfather of actors Auk and Per Aabel respectively. The main building was torn down and a smaller one was built. The old logs were used in the parson's new house, which today is Aabelheim Guesthouse. The Colonel's old storehouse remained standing on the property, where it still is today. When Aabel died in 1852, his daughter, Olin Christine, took over the house and lived there until she died in 1900.

It is uncertain just who lived in the house the succeeding years, but in 1942, Anna Jordan took over the property. In her youth, she had worked in the hotel business, and now she wanted to strike out on her own. She had no start capital, so she had to do everything herself. She set up a loom in the lounge, and for a year, she sat and wove tablecloths, napkins, bed linens, towels, and other things needed for the hotel. In 1943, together with her brother-in-law, Endre Undersell, she opened Aabelheim Guest-house, named after the parson.

The first years, Anna and Endre ran the guesthouse together, but after a while, Anna assumed the responsibility alone. Even though it had only five beds in the beginning, it was hard to run. The kitchen had a wood-burning stove and only cold water, but Anna was a good cook, and Aabelheim became known for its excellent kitchen. It was especially popular with sports fishermen and their families. The guesthouse rented a river, so they had their own fishing rights, and the trout bit willingly and often. Anna expanded little by little, and converted the barn and hayshed into a cozy annex.

Aabelheim is a small building influenced by an architectural style often used in the houses of senior civil servants and wealthy people at the beginning of the 1800's. The house is surrounded by a lovely garden.

The large main building at Vangen Motel has evolved through a long building process. The Neo-Classical portal in front of the oldest part has retained its old seats (below).

At the beginning of the 1970's, Anna's son, Ingmund Stigen, and his wife, Gurid, took over the guesthouse. Gurid had helped her mother-in-law for many years already, and now she carried on the traditions established by Anna. Gurid also became a popular hostess. As time went by, there were fewer fish in the river, and the fishermen began to go elsewhere. But tourists took their place. In 1995, son Arvid took over, so it's his turn to greet guests at the little white Hansel and Gretel house with multi-paned windows and lace curtains surrounded by a lush apple garden with an old stone border and flagstone paths, now a heritage building.

Vangen Motel

Vangen Motel, also run by Arvid Stigen, is just a few meters from Aabelheim Guest House.

It was once the home of Captain Mathias Juell. He died, however, in 1814, and in 1849, the property was sold to Knut Rosendahl. Knut had noticed hordes of brisling in the fjord, large catches, but not enough salt was available. He saw a source of income here! In 1847, he applied to the Aurland aldermen for a business license. He received it, and when he took over Captain Juell's house two years later, he opened a country store.

In 1853, Knut sold both property and business to Hans Johannes Brun. Brun expanded the house, and now the groundwork was laid for a hotel, a courthouse, trade, post and shipping offices at Vangen. He retained the country store, which Knut had started in the cellar of the old Juell house. The house was originally a one-story dwelling, but he raised the roof and added a floor.

The sitting room at Aabelheim.

Shortly thereafter, he built a new house on the north side, which later was connected with the old house. At that time, English tourists began to come to Aurland to hunt reindeer and fish salmon. For that reason, the new addition was called the English building, and the hotel at Vangen was established.

When Brun died in 1886 at the age of 60, the hotel, bakery, post and telegraph offices were sold to Ellend Wangen and his wife Stina. By this time, both Norwegian and foreign tourists had discovered wild and beautiful western Norway, and in the years ahead, the number of tourists coming to Aurland increased. This meant successful years for Ellend and Stina, who ran the hotel until after World War II.

For some years, the hotel was closed due to lack of fire insurance. At the beginning of the 1970's, owner Paul Ohnstad, began a comprehensive modernization and restoration of the venerable old building. In 1975, it was reopened as a motel, which it still is today.

Tourist destination Aurland

Aurland is one of the most popular tourist destinations in the area of Sogn og Fjordane. The area includes Aurland, Flåm, Gudvangen and Undredal and is centrally located by the new ferry-free road between Oslo and Bergen. The famous Aurland valley stretches from Vassbygdi via Hol in Hallingdal up to Geiteryggen mountain at the water divide toward Hallingdal. The valley is a wonderful place for hikers.

A detail from Aabelheim.

It is also possible to reach Aurland by train. The Flåm Railroad, which opened in 1941, traverses a steep, narrow and beautiful mountain valley and is a masterpiece of the engineer's art. It is only 20 kilometers long, but the trip from Myrdal station, which lies 867 meters above sea level, down to Flåm station by the Aurlandfjord takes about 45 minutes.

There are many sights in Aurland. Vangen church, an beautiful Gothic stone church from 1202, is located at Aurlandsvangen, while Undredal church is still the smallest church in use in Scandinavia. The county features a number of mountain dairy farms, and Aurland is known for its goat cheese. The Aurland shoe (a camel-colored shoe similar to a penny loafer) is also well-known. It is produced only a stone's throw from Aabelheim Guesthouse and Vangen Motel, old houses which also are among the regions finest tourist attractions.

In the pace of 100 years, the only changes on the exterior of Aabelheim's listed main building is a new dormer and a little more decoration on the entry portal. Photo: H. Vreim, National office of Historic Monuments archives.

Two fine old homes

Both Aabelheim and Wangen Motel were patterned after majestic larger buildings with roots in the official residences of the 18th century. The homes of wealthy bourgeoisie in Bergen served as models for the architecture in western Norway until late in the 19th century.

Aabelheim is probably the elder of the two houses, built in 1752. Colonel Jacob Gerhard Meidell was the first to live here. After Ole Aabel, a minister, purchased the property in 1822, he was supposed to have built a new house, but it is possible that he only added onto the old one. Parts of the interior, in any case, several 18th-century doors with high relief, indicate that older elements in the house were, at least, reused. Exterior details of the windows and entrance portal conform to the style in western Norway in the 1820's and 1830's-

According to a description from 1863, the house consisted of a corridor with an attic staircase, a kitchen with a large open fireplace and a pantry in the center of the house. There was a living room and a smaller bedroom at each end. This arrangement probably dates from the time of the original construction. The attic floor contained one room at the southern end, otherwise the rest was open. The small dormer over the main entrance was probably added around 1900 in connection with the furnishing of several rooms in the attic. The three set pieces over the portal frame with the two hanging arches in between cannot be seen in older photographs of the house and are probably copied from other older houses in the district after 1940.

This small building was made into a rooming house in 1943 and is well preserved. The layout is still the same, but the opening between the dining room and an earlier bedroom has been enlarged. For a while, there were plans to build a complete second floor or a new building alongside. But the buildings were placed on the list of historic monuments in 1941, and additional space was gained with the remodeling of a small annex in 1949. A small red-painted storehouse from Colonel Meidell's time is also part of this harmonious group of houses.

Wangen Motel's main building is much larger, but it also has seen major alterations over the years. Captain Mathias Juell's one-story house built in 1772 is preserved as the southern part of the present building. Merchant H.J. Brun bought the property in 1853 and had a general store in the cellar until he built a new shop closer to the fjord in the 1860's. Brun extended the house to two complete floors, and one of the upstairs rooms was referred to as Bailiff's Hall in 1867. Undoubtedly, the tax collector used this room as his office when he was in Aurland on official business.

Quite soon after he bought the property, Brun built a new house alongside the old. This house is now the first floor of the northern part of the main building. It was originally one floor with central dormers on both long sides and was connected to the older building with a small passage. Right from the beginning, this house had a terrace on the facade. English salmon fishermen and reindeer hunters used to sit here and enjoy the view of the fjord. For that reason, the house was called the "English building." A fire insurance description from 1867, mentioned specifically that many rooms here had gilded molding under the cornice, which indicates that such decoration was both unusual and costly at that time.

The two houses were each decorated with elegant Classical Revival style portals with semi-columns, joisting and a skylight, which was typical for Bergen architecture at the beginning of the 1800's. It was obviously built after other styles had become popular in the city and is an example of how the country districts could be many years behind the larger centers in stylistic development. All the same, the portals are valuable elements in the architecture and tell of glorious days long gone.

Brun's operations were considerable and covered trade, a guesthouse, a tannery, a dyehouse, farm, steamship office and many large quayside warehouses. There was also a school and a little tower building with a dovecote. After Brun went bankrupt in 1897, the farmhouses became Wangen Hotel. Eventually, the English building was extended to two complete floors and connected with the old main building to become the long structure which stands today. When the motel was opened in 1975, showers had been installed in the guest bedrooms, but otherwise, the fine molding and original doors were retained. A lounge is now furnished with both rustic and refined antiques.

The old portals are still main elements in the facade, along with the original terraces and the stone steps. The older portal has retained its old benches with Classical Revival style wrought iron legs. On the farm side are a number of buildings, including the shop, the dovecote and the storehouse. Along with their neighbor, Aabelheim, they help to recreate the atmosphere of the past.

FLEISCHER´S HOTEL

Voss

Sold the church and bought a hotel

In the 18th century, there were simple inns and guesthouses at Voss. Strategically located between two of the most famous fjords in the world, Sognefjord and Hardangerfjord, and only a short distance from Bergen, this beautiful rural area, then as now, was an important traffic junction for everyone who wanted to experience the wild and wonderful west country.

Today, Voss is western Norway's second largest tourist center, after Bergen. The comfortable inland climate, with snowy winters and warm summers, as well as a beautiful and varied landscape,

makes Voss an attractive year-round destination. Steep mountain-sides, many ski-lifts, well-prepared alpine slopes in all degrees of difficulty, and wide open spaces with kilometer after kilometer of cross-country skiing trails, have made Voss one of Norway's most popular winter resorts. But Voss is also popular with lovers of the great outdoors all summer. The center of the district, Vossevangen, at the end of Vang Lake, is surrounded by majestic mountains, green hillsides, glittering lakes, rivers and steep waterfalls. And Fleischer's Hotel, an institution in Norwegian and west country tourism, stands like a fairy tale castle in the middle of Vossevangen.

The first Fleischer comes to Voss
The Fleischer name has been connected with Voss since the middle of the 18th century. Johan Sechman Fleischer was born and bred in Denmark, but after a short military career, he left the navy, became a lawyer and was appointed district magistrate in Norway in 1733. He came to Voss in 1760, when the magistrate's office for Voss, Hardanger and Lysekloster was moved from Kinsarvik to Voss. Johan moved into Grovendal house, which still is in the Fleischer family. He acquired quite a lot of property in the area, and at his death in 1789, his eldest son inherited a fortune. At that time, the Danish-Norwegian king sold the country's churches to private people in order to finance his wars, and in that way, Fleischer acquired four churches in Voss. The son inherited them along with farms, large tracts of land and cash.

The hotel adventure begins
Even though the Fleischer family was by now well-established in Voss, more than 100 years passed before the family became involved in the profession for which the name is known – hotel management. The magistrate's great grandchild, Fredrik Lyth Ørum Fleischer, established the first Fleischer's Hotel in Voss. Born in 1835, he grew up at Lekve farm and became a surveyor. As a youth, he went to sea, and for several years, he traveled the world, spending some years in America, where he participated in the Civil War. During that time, he became interested in hotel management. This interest laid the foundation for one of Norway's most famous hotels.

When his father died in 1864, Fredrik returned to Voss, settled on Kapellan farm and began to receive travelers.

Voss is famous for smoked lamb heads, always on the menu at Fleischer's.

Fleischer's Hotel is known for its huge lunch buffet. It is served in front of the old buffet niche, which is still preserved, as is much of the old dining room interior (right).

The churches are sold

Meanwhile, Fredrik was not the only one interested in running a hotel at Voss. The area's first professional baker, Sebastian Jersin, already had a bakery, general store and hotel! In 1857, he built a large two-story building on his property, Basteryggen, where he took in guests. When a permanent coaching station was established at Voss five years later, he became its administrator, and he served as postmaster until his death in 1864. The hotel was called Vossevangen Hotel and Station.

When Sebastian Jersin died, Fredrik Lyth Ørum Fleischer purchased the entire property. He was able to raise the money by selling Voss church, which had been handed down in the family for four generations, to the municipality. Together with his wife, Magdalena Margrethe (nee Schlanbusch), he continued all operations, but he renamed the hotel Fleischer's Hotel. Fredrik and Magda, as she preferred to be called, developed the hotel into one of the best in the area. Magda was in charge of the kitchen. The stream of travelers increased slowly but surely, and by the beginning of the 1870's, the hotel was becoming too small. A two-story annex, the Vetle building, was built wall to wall with the original hotel.

the largest for miles around. It was a fantastic hotel, with 70 guest bedrooms. All the craftsmen were finished with their work, the carpenters and painters had made their final touches, and the only thing remaining was to remove a pile of sawdust and other trash. That's when the catastrophe took place. The trash self-combusted, and the beautiful wooden building was reduced to ashes in a few hours. Fredrik Lyth Ørum Fleischer witnessed his life's work go up in flames. Completely beside himself with despair, he saw both his fortune and his future in ruins. And he had not bought any fire insurance!

"Magda," he said to his wife. "We are ruined! We have lost everything!" But Magda comforted her husband. She was a practical woman and had kept the accounts during construction. Of course, she had purchased fire insurance!

"Fleischer's Improvised Hotel"

It was just a matter of starting all over again. The first problem at hand was to find rooms for all the tourists with reservations for the summer season. Magda and Fredrik rented the local school and called it, with gallows humor, "Fleischer's Improvised Hotel." Even though it wasn't exactly the most luxurious accommodation in the world, the guests got a roof over their heads.

Then they started rebuilding the hotel. With the same architect and the same craftsmen, work progressed quickly, and in 1889, the new hotel, almost exactly like the one which had been destroyed the previous year, was ready. Many predicted that the new hotel would be the ruin of the Fleischer family – it was too big and luxurious. But they were wrong, and tourists continued to visit the beautiful wooden palace which became one of the best hotels in the land.

Royal guests

European aristocracy and royalty soon discovered Fleischer's Hotel. Oscar II visited in 1872, while Crown Prince, and King Edward of England, then the Prince of Wales, visited Voss in 1885. Once the new and comfortable hotel was ready, even more royalty came. Kaiser Wilhelm II of Germany stayed here in 1890, 1894 and 1896. In 1894, he was accompanied by Empress Augusta Victoria. King Leopold of Belgium was at Fleischer's in 1896 and 1900, and King Oscar II returned in 1896. In 1898, then crown prince, later King Gustav of Sweden visited, and in 1903, Queen Margherita of Italy stayed at the hotel with a large retinue. The

From ashes to grand hotel

Development continued. Until this time, most tourists came by horse and carriage, but on July 11, 1883, the first train, drawn by a coal-burning locomotive, arrived at Voss. Even though it went through 48 tunnels and took four hours from Bergen to Voss, it connected Voss to the rest of the world forever. And with the connection to Norway's second largest city, also an important harbor, a new era in travel began. Fleischer's Hotel was once again was too small, and once again, Fredrik decided to build. But this time, he planned a big hotel.

On May 13, 1888, a fine, new Fleischer's Hotel was ready. With its 100-meter-long facade facing the lake, the building was

most exotic visitor was King Chulalongkorn and the Princes of Siam, who came with an enormous entourage in 1907. The following summer, in 1908, both Princess Margherita of Murat of France and King Friedrich of Sachsen visited Fleischer's. That same year, our own King Haakon was a guest there for the first time. He returned in 1909, 1914 and 1924. Another prominent guest was Queen Wilhelmina of the Netherlands. In 1928, she came with her daughter, Crown Princess Juliana, who also visited the hotel after she had become queen.

New generations take over
Between all these royal visits, life was busy as usual at Fleischer's. Fredrik and Magda had three children, Johan Sechman, Theodor Gerhard and Cecilia Susanna Ørum. After Fredrik died in 1906,

The beautiful scenery of western Norway provided the foundation for hotels at Voss. The terrace overlooks Vang lake and lush green hillsides (above).

A portrait of the first Fleischer at Voss, Johan Seckman Fleischer, hangs over the fireplace. It was painted by the famous Danish portrait artist, Jens Juell, in 1779.

Johan and Theodor took over the hotel. Both had studied hotel management in France, and they were helped by their mother, who had many years of experience. Tourism in Voss blossomed as never before and reached its apex with the opening of the Bergen Railroad. On November 27, 1909, the first passenger train left Kristiania and headed west. At Voss, eastern and western Norway were united by the Voss and Bergen railroads. "The Bergen Railroad is our generation's great achievement," declared King Haakon, honored guest on board.

This was a time of many new technical achievements and discoveries, and with these came increasing demands for comfort in the hotel trade. The Fleischer brothers made many changes and installed electric lights. In 1917, they decided to sell the hotel so they would have more time for their horses. A corporation, with John Walter as its director, took over the hotel, but retained both its name and reputation. Travelers still flocked to the hotel in 1928, when the brothers bought it back. Theodor and his son, Fredrik, managed the hotel. Fredrik had dreamed of taking over Fleischer's Hotel since childhood. Even after it was sold, he still held onto his dream, the main reason his father and uncle bought it back. Fredrik studied hotel management abroad, and after his father died in 1935, he took over the family firm. In 1937, he began a comprehensive renovation, and when the hotel opened for the summer season in 1939, it was as modern and comfortable as a hotel could be for its time.

War and peace

Less than a year later, the Second World War broke out. The Germans wanted to destroy the important junction at Voss, and on April 24 and 25, 1940, the area was bombed and almost all of Vossevangen was leveled. As if by a miracle, Fleischer's Hotel escaped destruction. The bomb, which was supposed

The hosts at Fleischer's, Gerd and Olaf Fleischer Tønjum, along with their son, Jan Fredrik Tønjum, who is in line to take over this traditional family hotel.

to destroy the venerable wooden palace, remained undetonated in the garden outside. Nonetheless, it was impossible to run the hotel in a normal way during the following five years. The Germans took over the hotel, and for the duration of the war, the best rooms were used by high-ranking officers. During one period, Fleischer's Hotel even was a soup station for German soldiers.

But the beautiful old building was allowed to remain unspoiled. After peace came in 1945, tourists returned, and Fredrik continued to run the hotel as his predecessors had done before him, until he died in 1957, only 60 years old.

Fleischer's Hotel today

Fredrik was a bachelor and childless, so when he died, his nephew, Olaf Fleischer Tønjum, took over the hotel. He had studied hotel management in Switzerland and was working at Hotel Bristol in Bergen when he heard of his uncle's death. Even though he

wanted to gain more experience before taking over the family business, he could do nothing more than return to Voss. He was only 24, and a great task awaited. The hotel had not been renovated since 1939, and it was rundown. New and modern guest bedrooms were needed, and the first thing Olaf did was to build a new wing onto the old wooden building. The annex, which was ready in 1959, added 18 new and modern rooms to the hotel.

In 1966, Olaf married Gerd (nee Ohnstad) from Aurland in Sogn. She had worked as a tour guide in Voss, and with her lively personality, good humor and genuine concern for the guests, she developed into a perfect hostess. Even though it has been modernized frequently, the old wooden castle has retained its style and charm. And even though Fleischer's Hotel is a first class modern hotel with all the comforts, it is still run in the old manner. Just as their predecessors did, Gerd and Olaf Fleischer Tønjum take good care of their guests.

From an architectural viewpoint, Fleischer's Hotel is among the most elaborate of the old wooden hotels in Norway. Its architect was Peter Andreas Blix (1831-1901), who was educated in Germany, as were most Norwegian architects of the era. Before he designed the hotel at Voss, he worked for the railroad and had also built wonderful Gothic Revival villas. He eventually became even more popular designing restorations.

The elongated shape of the new hotel was determined by the lot, which was lodged between the main road and the railroad. For that reason, the hotel did not have any crosswings, as did most larger hotels at that time. The facades were composed as if constructed from many different shapes and towers

The main building from 1889 originally had a large open veranda in front of the dining room, which was quite typical of the times. A comparison with the competitors in the background shows that this was a large project, both in dimensions and in architectural design. Photograph: Knud Knudsen, about 1890, Bergen University Library.

A Norwegian-French "castle"

to achieve a great variation in the wall surfaces. This gives the impression of balanced asymmetry. Even the middle section with two towers, which at first looks symmetrical, was balanced with different shapes, placements and dimensions of verandas and windows. The dining room was built with a higher ceiling than the rest of the first floor, and that allowed for even more variation in the main facade. The facades have a definite verticality, with towers and dormers with sharp gables in different sizes and shapes, with and without verandas. The southwestern corner was broken by an added bay window topped with a slim tower. On top of all that, perforated combs were placed on the roof ridges and thin spires on the apexes of the gableboards and towers.

The shapes of the towers are rooted in medieval German and French castles. The shape of the gables, in which an arch is inserted into the gable triangle and is supported by diagonal struts into the wall, is an old French form found in half-timbered houses from the late Middle Ages all over northern France, especially in Normandy. In France, where the origin of this shape is well-known, the style is called "Neo-Norman" when it is used in historically inspired architecture during the 19th century.

The great variation of shapes expressed the Gothic Revival ideal that a house should be planned from the inside out - not formed within a stated and regular shape. Fleischer's Hotel is a consistent and successful example of this ideal. The architect fully mastered the great volume of the building without any monotony resulting anywhere.

The building was painted so that constructions and details were emphasized in a darker color than that used in the paneled wall surfaces. According to the ideals of the time regarding wooden architecture, the colors were supposed to suit the materials. That meant that yellow walls with brown constructions became very popular.

The new hotel had 120 beds and room for 200 in the dining room, a really big hotel back then. Inside, it was adorned with heavy beam constructions and

cornices, impressive doors and high wainscoting with wood carving in the dining room, reception area and in the garden lounge. The wainscoting in the garden lounge and in the reception area is quite like that of Bergen Cathedral, which had been restored by architect Blix a few years earlier. The focal point in the dining room, then as now, is a portal-framed niche with a serving counter with a tall buffet behind, inspired by the trend-setting designers of the day in England and in Germany. Inside, only staining and oil was used, so the structure of the wood would remain visible, while decorative painting was limited to molding and carvings. Additional decoration includes stenciled leaves and vines which still can be seen in what today is the bar.

The furnishings in the common rooms were relatively simple, with refectory tables in the dining room and, for the most part, light furniture in the salons, supplemented with a few sitting groups with upholstered armchairs and sofas. A furniture suite in plush fabric in a combination of Renaissance Revival and other historic styles, accompanied by the obligatory potted palm, had pride of place in the lounge, as well. The original furniture was replaced little by little, but some older pieces are still in use in two of the lounges, which feature 18th century portraits on the walls. Antique furniture, some dating from the earliest days of the hotel, can now be seen in the corridors on the upper floors.

The hotel has been altered and extended, all according to the changing needs and ideals of the times. The guest bedrooms has been improved considerably, for the original standard was quite Spartan, from a modern point of view. One of the larger building projects was the remodeling of the original open veranda in front of the dining room. It was extended and remodeled in stages, eventually enclosed in glass and incorporated into the dining room. In later years, the garden room and smokers' lounge were joined to make a larger bar. By then, the old style of the hotel had once again become popular, so the original wainscoting was repaired and extended to include the bar counter.

The most important alteration was the eastern addition, which was completed in 1959. In those days, the ideals of the time demanded that it reflect the modern idiom, and it did that to the fullest. It was a large, rectangular, monotonous concrete block in so-called modern style, which in no way even tried to utilize the shapes and variations of the original building. This concrete building was expanded and remodeled in 1994 to include an additional floor with steep roof and pointed dormers, so it functions better with the old wooden building. A corner tower was added on the railroad side and the entire building was sided with old-fashioned wooden panels. Inside, some of the characteristic door frames from the old building have been copied in the new, thus providing continuity between the two. The architect who accomplished this was Per Gaare, who also designed the swimming hall and the course and conference center in the 1970's. This was positioned close to the ground in front of the old wooden building, so that the roof could form a terrace in front of the dining room and lounges. At the same time, it shields the hotel from the traffic on the main road.

In spite of all the changes through the years, Fleischer's Hotel is still an important monument to the wooden architecture of the 19th century — a paraphrase over a French castle from the late Middle Ages which, with its combination of different shapes, is unique in Norwegian wooden architecture. Restoration and refurbishing has been done in keeping with the original style of the hotel. This is a place to experience a big hotel of the "Belle Époque" of tourism, the time just before the First World War.

JAUNSEN GUESTHOUSE
Granvin

A hotel for country folks

The idyllic settlement of Eide is the center of Granvin munici-pality. Its central location at the heart of Granvinfjord makes it an ideal starting point for excursions in Hardanger, the beautiful district that is often called Norway's orchard. A ten minute ferry ride from Bruravik to Brimnes brings you to Eidfjord and wild and dramatic Måbødalen, the gateway to the largest mountain plateau in Northern Europe, Hardangervidda. The 182-meter Vøringsfoss waterfall is at Måbødalen, as well as the recently opened Hardangervidda Nature Center, a colorful adventure center which tells about Hardangervidda and the inner fjord region. Eide is only 25 minutes by car from Voss.

But the settlement of Eide is an attraction in itself. Eide has taken special care of its old building traditions, especially down by the pier, with its unique wooden architecture. And right in the middle of all this, along National Route 7 is traditional Jaunsen Guesthouse.

From the beginning, it was called Graven Song's Guesthouse, and was both a guesthouse and a general store. The first owner we can identify was Mads Rasmusson from Bergen, who had the guesthouse license for Eide from 1666 until he died in 1678. He also ran a lumber yard and a sawmill. After his death, his heirs demanded that the house be moved from Eide to Bergen, but because the estate owed 10 riksdaler in rent, the bailiff forbade this.

The Pyck family
Olav Olavson Pyck took over both the guest-house and the store around 1710. He also owned a boat which he used to transport planks, birch bark, and vegetable fibers to Bergen.

Olav and his wife were childless, but despite this, the guesthouse at Eide remained in Pyck family ownership until 1852. Hans Johannes-son Pyck, a relative from Tysnes, received the King's license to operate a guesthouse in 1753. In addition to the guesthouse, he had several farms, with three cotters' farms attached, and a sawmill. He was hard working and industrious, and he established, among other things, the

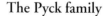

The antique furniture is right at home in the fine salon. This room has been reverently restored, as have the others in the house. Note the well-preserved, richly designed Baroque door in the background.

trade center at Eide. Eventually, he had eight children, and to add to his income, he fished for herring each spring.

His son, Jan Top Hansson Pyck, received the guesthouse license in 1785 and took over the place. He was a hard-working man, just like his father, but he was also a shrewd businessman, not especially popular among the locals. He owned a sawmill and two farms in Kongstun, which now surround the present guesthouse. He also built a large new house which later became Jaunsen's Hotel. Jan was a bachelor, thus childless, and therefore left all his properties to a nephew, Rikoll Ivarsson Eide.

Rikoll took the name Kongstun, from the farm he inherited from his uncle. He was only 19 years old when took over everything, but he had been apprenticed to his uncle and soon proved to be an able and honest businessman. His widow, Kristi Ivarsdotter Folkedal, got full rights to the estate when Rikoll died in 1850. And it was no small estate! Rikoll was the richest man in Hardanger, and Kristi inherited an estate valued at 120,000 crowns. Later, she sold the guesthouse to Andreas Severin Jaunsen.

Jaunsen's Hotel

Andreas was the son of a Bergen ship broker, who had managed the trade center at Granvin for Kristi Kongstun, Rikoll's widow. In 1858, he was granted permission to open a general store, and a year later he accepted the deed for "numerous houses and lots" from the widow. In 1861, he took over both the rural post office and the steamship office after Rikoll Kongstun. The general store and the guesthouse were run the same as before, and Andreas was both respected and popular among the locals. In 1857, he married Ivarine Georgine Müller from Bergen, who had come to Granvin as a housekeeper. They had three children, and in 1885, the eldest son, Severin, took over the business from his father.

That same year, all the buildings on the steamship quay were destroyed by a great fire. This included the general store, the warehouse, a boat house, and a large warehouse which belonged. After this, Severin took over the post office and became a steamship clerk for the Hardanger Sunnhordland Steamship Company, while the general store was closed. The guesthouse was renamed Jaunsen's Hotel. Severin was married to Madli Olavsdotter Tveito, a very talented cook. They ran the hotel together until 1920, when they decided to close this bastion of tradition. Severin died in 1926 and Madli in 1936. The inheritance was then divided, and what previously had been the hotel was used as a house.

The buildings at Jaunsen Guesthouse have stood as they do today for over 200 years.

The lounge in the Jaunsen house has a beamed ceiling, and the walls have retained their original covering. Some lovely pieces of furniture have followed the house through the many generations.

The hotel's original main door, with its heavy Baroque design, leads from the glass veranda to the entry hall.

From a house to a guest house

In 1990, 70 years after the business was closed, Severin Jaunsen's granddaughter Randi decided that she wanted to try to breathe life into the old guesthouse traditions. Together with her sister-in-law Ragna, she dreamed of renovating the old building so that it again could be used as a hotel. They soon realized that it need thorough renovation and restoration. They went out into the community for financing, and on July 10, 1991, they founded the Jaunsen Guesthouse Corporation. As many as 40 shareholders from Granvin contributed money to fix up the hotel.

It took three years to restore the hotel. They worked in close cooperation with the Hordaland county conservator, and all work was done according to specific guidelines for restoration. Finally, on June 11, 1994, the old hotel once again opened its doors.

Today, the 40 local shareholders still own the hotel, so it is literally the people's hotel. To ensure proper management, they have leased the place to a professional manager from Bergen, Otto Stenhjelm. He and his wife, Solfrid, run a cozy guesthouse with a relaxed atmosphere and traditional Norwegian food.

The coastal settlement of Eide in Granvin has been a communication center for traffic from Hardanger overland to Voss as long as anyone can remember. The change from sea to land transport still can be seen. There are still railroad tracks from the Voss-Hardanger line, which had its end station here, and for a time, provided a foundation for the growth of the area. Even in the 1600's, the local guesthouse was described as "ancient." The buildings which still serve as the guesthouse are very old and valuable, even if they do not date from the earliest time. They are part of a larger milieu with many old houses, some of which are well preserved and are worth examining in depth.

Originally, there were probably small-paned windows. The present type of window, with larger panes, usually dates from around the middle of the 19th century.

A steep old staircase leads from the small entry up to the guestrooms. Doors of different periods open onto the rooms on the main floor. The door leading into the former kitchen at the back, now a den with a fireplace, probably dates from the time the house was built, as do doors and doorframes in many other parts of the house. In the big reception room, the firewall flanked by two doors is a fine example of Bergen style carpentry work in the last half of the 18th century. The frames with their roundels with broken lines are typical of the Baroque style.

century and a chandelier from around 1930, 150 years of furniture styles are represented here. An impressive Renaissance Revival suite of furniture, veneered in mahogany and covered with patterned red plush, reigns in the formal reception room. The guest bedrooms in this building are much as they were before, and the fine old molding has been retained, while at the same time, new bathrooms have been installed.

For the reopening of the guesthouse in 1994, the courthouse and the Jaunsen house were connected with a small building to make a new entrance and reception area. Once again, travelers can experience the traditional old buildings, parts of which have

Reverently restored in the Baroque style

Of the guesthouse's three buildings, the simple peasant cottage farthest east dates from 1726. It houses the kitchen and has been altered considerably inside. Earlier, farmers and people from the area stayed here and did not mix with the civil servants and upper-class folks in the other buildings. Close to the peasant cottage is a courthouse with its two-story end wall facing the road. In earlier days, when the chief magistrate traveled through the district, he held court here for both civil disputes and criminal cases. Earlier, it was located down by the quay, where it also was used as a guesthouse as early as 1674. In 1825, it was moved to its present location. In the passage outside, the fine treatment of the notched logs in the house's original outer wall is still visible. Inside, the log walls have been overcut and are covered with modern panels.

The so-called Jaunsen house, with lounges downstairs and three guestrooms in the old style upstairs, is even better preserved and still has many of its original furnishings. This was Jaunsen's Hotel until 1920. The exact age of the house is unknown, but different details in the older doors and their frames date from about 1760-1790 and point to a date of construction toward the end of that period. Enterprising Jan Top Hansson Pycks took over the guesthouse in 1785, a likely date for building. The entrance at the center of the house has a portal in the Baroque style. With its curved shapes and bulbous lower door panels, it still stands inside the glass veranda which was added about 100 years later.

Many pieces of fine furniture are in the lounges. In the largest room is a large mirror of approximately the same age as the house, along with a somewhat younger Empire secretary in mahogany veneer, either northern German or Danish, or perhaps even made by the proficient cabinetmakers in Bergen. The Pseudo-Rococo sofa dates from the last half of the 19th century, as does the tall stepped stove. With a corner cupboard and chairs in Biedermeier, table in Renaissance Revival, chairs from the first half of this

Jaunsen's Hotel was written on the facade, and a new reception area has been constructed in the space between two buildings. Otherwise, the exterior is still the original. Photograph: Ant. J. Karlsen, 1905, National Office of Historic Monuments archives.

been unusually well preserved. In addition, they have been refurbished carefully and have been furnished with antiques which have stayed with them for generations.

SANDVEN HOTEL
Norheimsund

From a crofter's cottage to a hotel with its own waterfall

Sandven Hotel, in the beautiful Hardanger settlement of Norheimsund, is about an hour's drive from Bergen. In the old days, two crofter's cottages belonged to Sandven farm, and one was on the site of the present hotel, which was where it all began. Young, industrious Nils Sjursen Skutlaberg lived there, and as was the custom in those days, he took the name of the farm where he lived, Sandven. But Nils was not satisfied with running a farm. He had learned to sail, so he rented a boat and went to Bergen with butter, meat and hides, which area farmers wanted to sell. He returned with boatloads of city goods. Business was booming, and Nils could sell an entire boatload in a day.

Until 1842, being in trade was considered a city privilege, and therefore, it was difficult for Nils to get an official trading license. The local council was afraid that people would spend their money on useless things and "ruin themselves." But the laws regulating trade were changed, and Nils Sandven received his royal license signed by six cabinet ministers. He was obligated to maintain a courtroom, be a shipping agent for the postal steamship, "to keep the place stocked with the necessary wares," and to provide travelers with "necessary and good lodging."

The bailiff had recommended Nils for the license. Both he and the district magistrate were dissatisfied with the old arrangement, in which the parsonage was used as both courthouse and guesthouse. Nils knew what was demanded of him with regard to comfort and service, and he realized that he had to build a new house to accommodate his guests.

Sandven is still an important center of communication in Hardanger. The restored dockside warehouse in the foreground has been part of the property since the mid-1800's, when business activities were more important than the hotel.

From coaching station to shipping office

In 1858, a new two-story guesthouse was built on the site of the old crofter's cottage. Nils built a courthouse alongside, and the old general store, which he had established in 1845, now gained a new floor and was connected to the dockside warehouse built in 1851. The latter is still standing and now houses a arts and crafts shop.

Guests soon arrived, including businessmen, civil servants and tourists. Some returned year after year, among them the famous violinist and composer Ole Bull. He often stood on the hotel stairs and played for guests and village residents. Other times, he climbed to the top of Grautaberg hill, where he stood and played and let the rhapsodic sounds of his violin float over the area, so that "many eyes became misty and tears fell."

At that time, courthouse and inn usually were combined, and now the parsonage also lost the inn to Nils Sandven. The civil servants demanded travel connections, and here everything was arranged precisely according to occupation and rank. Bailiff and magistrate were supposed to have 13 men to row the boat, the bishop, eight, and the dean of several parishes, four, while the parson and sheriff had to make do with two men.

After a while, the steamship took over transportation needs. In 1846, the first steamship was seen on the Hardangerfjord, and in 1854, the "Patriot" began a scheduled route. It did not stop at Norheimsund, however, but once the 90-foot long paddle steamer "Vøring" arrived, Norheimsund became a scheduled stop. The word "stop" can be interpreted in more than one way. The boat was out in the fjord, and Nils Sandven had to row out to fetch and deliver passengers and freight. For fear of fire, steamships were not allowed to dock at the quay the first years.

The dining room is one of the country's best preserved from the turn of the century. It is more richly decorated with carvings and stenciled designs than most.

A new generation – a new hotel

Early on, "Vøring" came to Norheimsund every eighth day. The other paddle steamer, "Bjørnen," did the same. In 1869, a new and larger ship, "Hardangeren," began to traffic the fjord. It stopped at Norheimsund twice a week and could also dock at the quay. People could go right on land and walk the few meters to the hotel. This, of course, contributed to an increase in tourist traffic.

These were busy times for Nils Sandven. He had a hotel, a general store and a shipping office. In addition, he was a founder of Vikøy Savings Bank, where he was cashier for 22 years, and when Norheimsund got its own post office, he became postmaster.

In 1875, his son, Nils Nilson Sandven, took over the properties. The number of tourists was increasing and he saw the need for additional and more comfortable rooms. The old building was torn down, and in 1896-1897, he built the large hotel which is still standing today. At the same time, he filled up the beach below the hotel and made a small but beautiful park with weeping birch, exotic plants, and tables and benches where guests could sit and enjoy the view of the fjord, mountain and powerful Folgefonna falls. He also built a large floating wharf, where there were rowboats for the guests and where the launches from the tourist ships docked.

The largest lounge houses one of the hotel's best preserved old interiors furnished with antiques and old furniture.

The Hardanger region has rich handicraft and applied art traditions. The Hardanger bunad (regional folk costume) is intricately decorated, and Hardanger embroidery and the Harding fiddle are well-known outside the region as well (below).

An active host

Many tourists at Norheimsund came to see what Kaiser Wilhelm had seen, Østhusfoss waterfall, later called Steinsdalsfoss. Nils Sandven saw possibilities here. He bought the entire waterfall and built a dragon style bridge right by it. He sat there guarding it and collected 10 øre from each person crossing over to visit the cafe and buy refreshments.

Nils liked new inventions and built a private electric power station which provided light for the hotel long before the station at Kaldestad was built in 1914. He had the first car in the county, and Norheimsund Bus Company, which he established, lived on in Kvam Bus Company, Hardanger Bus Company and today, Hardanger and Sunnhordland Steamship Company. In 1890, he founded Vikør's Telephone Company and had the telephone exchange at Sandven until 1934.

In the early 1920's, Nils' nephew, Nils Oleson Sandven, took over. The years during and after the First World War had been difficult, and the tourists had stayed home. But once again, traffic was increasing, and in 1925, Nils had to expand the hotel. The roads had been improved and many more people found their way to this beautiful place on the Hardangerfjord. Even though there was competition from "floating hotels," cruise ships, he still had enough to do. The passengers had to go over land to see the falls.

Sandven Hotel today

In 1951, Nils Oleson Sandven passed the hotel to the fourth generation, Ola N. Sandven, who ran the hotel, with mixed results, until 1990. As time went by, the proud old wooden building had become more and more dilapidated, and it could not

satisfy demands for modern conveniences. Some felt it should be demolished, but the people of the area had strong feelings for the old hotel, which had been the center of the settlement for more than 100 years. "Sandven Cultural Hotel Foundation," owned by some inhabitants of Norheimsund, took over the hotel. From 1991 to 1993, there was hectic voluntary communal work on the hotel. Parts were refurbished, while at the same time, the foundation tried to keep the hotel running. This did not work, and in August, 1993, bankruptcy was a fact. The administrators wanted to divide the property and sell off the buildings separately, but luckily, the county curator in Hordaland stopped that. He declared a ban on partitioning, and in the end, the entire property was sold at a forced auction to the county late in 1993.

The county offered the place to hotelier Tron Bach from Finse. He had been a glacier guide, before he bought Hotel Finse, which he restored and managed for many years. He also was a founder of the Workers' Museum there. He accepted the offer from Kvam municipality and bought Sandven Hotel in April, 1994. In close cooperation with the County Curator, he began restoration. The kitchen and all fire hazards had to be replaced. On May 12, 1994, the noble hotel reopened its doors. The old dockside warehouse was refurbished and now houses the Nova arts and crafts shop, while the courthouse is a gallery showing works by Hardanger artists. Between these two houses is the proud hotel building – as it has been for 100 years – like a fairy tale castle by the Hardangerfjord.

The oldest part of Sandven Hotel includes remains of the first guesthouse on this site, built in 1858 in the local style influenced by the architecture of Bergen. In 1872, it was lengthened and modernized into a fashionable hotel in the style of the time. This meant large roof projections and the almost obligatory veranda with gable roof on the long wall facing the sea.

Different shapes from different times

This hotel building was again expanded, in all directions, and re-modeled into something completely different in 1896-1897. The result of this is the oldest part remaining today, with verandas, steep roofs and pointed gables. The architect was Anders Olavsson Steine (1862-1901), who was born and bred nearby but had completed his education as an architect in Hannover eight years earlier. The architecture at Sandven shows the clearly influence of the German wooden buildings of the time. At the same time, there are obvious Norwegian elements in the decoration.

As far as country hotel architecture from this period is concerned, Sandven Hotel is quite advanced compared to most others. Its complex ground plan gives the impression that the building is composed of many structural elements without symmetry, emphasized by the many verandas in different shapes and dimensions, which protrude on many sides to give the facades life and variation. Usually, this style is called "Swiss," but with the steep roofs and pointed gables, it is equally correct to speak of Gothic Revival. Before some minor alterations at the turn of the century, this aspect was even more evident, with many small pointed gables at the bottom of the large roof surfaces. These were later flattened out to allow for larger windows and more space in attic rooms. The large gables over the verandas have ingenious beam constructions supplemented with curved shapes and give a very lively and decorative expression. This, too, is typical of Gothic Revival wooden architec-

Sandven Hotel as it stood after the renovations and additions in 1896-7. The shapes are varied and composed, with verandas in all directions. The large dining room, with its high ceiling, was placed in the new wing, on the left under the veranda, where the ladies stand with hats as wide as parasols.
Photograph: J. Karlsen, National Office of Historic Monuments archives.

ture. The rooftops are decorated with elements from the Norwegian dragon style, so popular at the time. This can be seen in the raised wooden combs along the ridges and in the dragon heads projecting from the gable apexes. These dragons might seem a little loose at the neck, but they are actually patterned after Heddal stave church in Telemark, which dates from the 13th century.

Three lounges were placed on the east side facing the sea. One still has its fine furnishings, with high wainscoting and decorative ceiling beams. Massive doors with strong frames in profiled molding and brown oil varnish, which allows the structure of the wood to be seen, also are part of the picture. Outside was a long, shady veranda, which later was partially enclosed.

The row of lounges ends with the dining room, placed at a right angle to the building, with its long wall facing south. As in many other hotels from this period, the ceiling is higher in this room than in the others on the same floor. Outside, the difference in height contributes to even more variation in the facades. The dining room was more lavishly decorated than usual, and it is now among the most decorative and best preserved from the time. It has great posts along the walls, a heavy cornice and roof beams, in addition to decorative wainscoting with painted leaf ornament in the upper panels. The gable triangle on the short wall between the two doors to the service area was decorated with intricate carvings of dragons, tendrils and leaves, typical for the dragon style. Norheimsund was a center for wood carving, so it is not surprising to find such carvings at this hotel. Under the carved gable in the dining room stood a built-in buffet, which was so important that it was mentioned separately in the first fire insurance policy.

This was a large, modern hotel when it was finished in 1897. On the attic floor were 18 guest rooms, and on the second floor, 16 rooms. It was so modern that it had a bathroom with both enameled tub and a wood-burning hot water heater.

In 1924, the hotel was expanded with a new kitchen and guest wing to the west, designed by Arnesen and Darre Kaarbø, one of the larger architect firms in Bergen. The wing was built in the Neo-Classical style of the 1920's, which is most clearly expressed in the proportions, the window frames and in the columnar portal on the end wall. A banquet hall was built on the south side in 1960, designed by Bergen architect Einar Vaardal-Lunde, in that period's mdernistic, rectangular shapes in concrete with vast surfaces in glass.

Over time, the entrance and the interiors in the oldest building were subjected to modernization and additions. In recent years, much of this has been removed or changed to harmonize better with the original. For subsequent renovation, the old building's original style serves as the model as can be seen in the new reception area with its coffee bar, designed by architect Per Gaare and interior decorator Ellen Hesthaug. Other buildings belonging to the hotel have also been renovated recently, including the old waterside warehouse with a shop and a boathouse from the beginning of the 18th century.

UTNE HOTEL
Utne

Living hotel history

At the north end of the Folgefonn peninsula, where Hardanger-fjord separates into three arms – Granvinfjord, Eidfjord and Sør-fjord – is the idyllic village of Utne. For years, this beautiful settlement has been a magnet for both Norwegian and foreign tourists. The fantastic landscape, with its powerful, snowclad peaks, and the blue-green Hardangerfjord, forms a beautiful frame around thousands of fruit trees – just as beautiful in the spring when they stand in full blossom, as in the fall, when their branches are weighed down with apples. It's a short distance from Utne to such fantastic natural wonders as Folgefonn and Vøringsfoss waterfalls. It's no wonder that painters, authors and composers found their way to Utne.

Down by the quay in the little village, surrounded by a beautiful garden enclosed with a white picket fence, and with a fantastic view of both fjord and mountains is one of Norway's oldest and best preserved wooden hotels – Utne Hotel.

A license instead of a salary
The hotel's history started in 1722. After 10 years of fighting, the Great Nordic War ended in 1720, and instead of pay, officer Peder Larsson Børsem from Strandebarm received a license from the king to run a guesthouse at Utne. Peder did not build a beautiful hotel. The entire guesthouse consisted of a living room, kitchen, hall and one bedroom. These rooms are still in use today, and Queen Sonja always stays in this particular bedroom, whenever she visits Utne Hotel.

The district court was at Utne from 1728, and traffic at the little guesthouse increased. But innkeeper Børsem died in 1735 at age 54, and his widow, Elisabeth Schrøder, from Bergen, took over. Five years later, she married Samson Torsteinson Samland, a smith. He preferred smithing to innkeeping, so when Elisabeth died in 1749, he had find a new fiancée so the place could have a proper hostess. He went to Vosse-vangen and became engaged to Trone Marie-

The history of the buildings at Utne Hotel stretches all the way back to the 1600's.

Ferry traffic on Hardangerfjord is an important part of life at Utne. The hotel is situated right by the quay (right).

In one of the rooms in the oldest part of the house, there is a spiral staircase up to the guest rooms on the second floor, which houses a glassed-in veranda from the 1870's.

The hotel dining room was built in 1930. The Renaissance cupboard from the 1600's served as the departure point for the furnishings (previous pages).

Blomberg, daughter of the innkeeper at Voss. Samson and Trone Marie never married, because Samson died just after the engagement. Luckily, an engagement was considered equal to a wedding in those days, so Trone Marie was approved as his "wife" and she continued as innkeeper. In 1755, she married Hans Hanssen Pyck, son of the innkeeper at Eide. They had many sons, but none was interested in taking over the inn. In 1785, the inn was sold to the family which still runs it today.

A fast-paced development

Johannes Sveinson Winess from Vines was a merchant with his own boat who had the right to sell all kinds of "necessities." A new epoch began when he bought the guesthouse. The village became the center of commerce for all of Inner Hardanger. Since he had little or no time to run the guesthouse, his wife, Sara, assumed the responsibility. Sara Johansdatter Brandt's father was the sexton in Kvam, and the family originally came from court circles in Flensburg. She brought silk brocade dresses and silk shoes with silver buckles to Utne. Eventually, silver spoons were made from the buckles, but the silver pearl necklace, which Sara always wore, is still in family.

When Johannes died in 1828, their son, Johan Brandt Winess, took over the guesthouse and received his license in 1829. That same year, an inn was established at Utne, with the innkeeper as stationmaster. In 1836, Hardanger got its first post office, also at Utne, and Johan became postmaster. He was in charge of postal transport between Eide and Utne until steamship traffic began in 1861. Then he took over as steamship agent at Utne. Eventually, scheduled traffic on the fjord increased, and Utne became the permanent junction between the boats in Inner Hardanger. This continued until cars took over, and Utne became a ferry landing.

"Mother Utne"

Johan married three times, last in 1832 with Torbjørg Johannesdotter Utne, the legendary Mother Utne. As a young girl, Torbjørg was in service with Sara at Utne. She was only 20, when she married Johan, and from then on, she took over both the work and the responsibility. At that time, in the middle of the 1830's, tourist traffic in western Norway was in its earliest stages. Those who came to Hardanger before this were more explorers than tourists. But when Dean Herzberg began to market Hardanger and especially Folgefonna abroad, and when Professor Hansteen "discovered" Vøringsfoss falls in 1821 and later made it famous, tourists began to arrive.

Utne Guesthouse quickly became the center for tourist traffic in Hardanger. One reason was its central location, but most of the honor is due Mother Utne herself. She was like a mother to the guests, and she really knew how to make them feel at home. In his book, "Ullensvang," O. Olafsen describes her like this: "She was more than just a good housekeeper, intelligent, careful, hard-working, ambitious, strict with others as with herself, but she understood how to spread well-being all around, she was made to be an innkeeper's wife. Everyone felt good with her, and Utne became a place which was visited more and more."

Torbjørg was Utne's hostess for 70 years. The inn eventually received hotel status, and increasing popularity forced her to expand. Guests returned year after year, mostly tourists from around the world, but also famous Norwegians, such as writer Per Christian Asbjørnsen, musician and composer Ole Bull, and painters Adolph Tidemand and Eilif Petersen. The latter painted the famous picture of Mor Utne which now hangs in the National Gallery in Oslo.

For over 50 years, Hildegun Aga Blokhus has been the hostess at Utne Hotel. She is often compared with her predecessor, Mother Utne.

Living hotel history

When Mother Utne died in 1902, her son sold the hotel to Anders Johannesson Utne. He ran it until 1918, when he sold it to lawyer Lars Aga and his wife Gurid. Lars Aga was the grandson of Mother Utne's sister and saw it as his life's work to recreate the good reputation the hotel enjoyed under his great-aunt. Lars and Gurid restored the hotel and in 1930, it was presented as a "modern" version of the traditional business.

In 1956, the Agas passed the place on to their daughter Hildegun and her husband, Olav Blokhus. Hildegun had, in practice, functioned as the hotel's hostess since 1942, because her mother was not well. Hildegun was widowed in 1965, but she continued to run the hotel alone for many years. She maintained all the old traditions. During her more than 50 years as hostess, she arranged a large buffet table with Norwegian specialties every Sunday lunch. She was there in her freshly pressed Hardanger regional costume, and at exactly five minutes before noon, she rang the bell to announce that lunch was served. When everyone was seated, she led the waitresses, all in regional dress, into the dining room carrying a large bowl of sour cream porridge. In both Norwegian and English, she explained how rømmegrøt is eaten with cinnamon-sugar, and she told about the hotel's other specialties. For many, especially foreign tourists, this was the high point of their stay at Utne, and at the same time, Hildegun gave the hotel a profile abroad. It is not without reason that she often has been compared with the legendary Mother Utne.

On January 1, 1996, Hildegun Aga Blokhus turned the hotel over to the Utne Hotel Foundation, which has been founded to preserve the historic hotel buildings and arrange for responsible management of the venerable hotel. Her dearest wish is that Utne Hotel also shall be run in the good old-fashioned way in the future and that the original surroundings will be preserved, so that the place can continue to be what it is today – living hotel history.

There is a Biedermeier furniture suite in the lounge from the time of legendary Mother Utne. On the wall above hangs Magnus Hardeland's copy of Eilif Peterssen's famous portrait of her.

tne Hotel is probably the oldest hotel in Norway which has been business uninterrupted. In addition, it is the hotel which has preserved most of its buildings and furnishings from its long history. The earliest guesthouse, from 1722, is the southeast part of the hotel building today. There is still a guest room in the corner of what originally was a living room. The oldest building also included the innermost half of the veranda lounge, where there now is a spiral staircase up to the second floor, and the outer half of the present fireplace lounge, originally a kitchen. This house probably was old when the guesthouse was established. There was a law court at Utne from 1728, and at that time, the two-story courthouse due south of the hotel was moved up to Utne from Jåstad, farther south in the fjord. This

The many types of doors from different times used inside give an idea of the different phases of construction and earlier modernization. The oldest date from the middle of the 18th century. The fireplace room features five generations of doors, from that time until far into the 20th century.

The interiors include furnishings from throughout the hotel's long history. In the corner by the fireplace, in the building's oldest section, are chairs in the national romantic dragon style from the beginning of the 20th century. Many Biedermeier style sitting groups date from Mother Utne's time. In the lounge is a mid-19th-century piano which Mother Utne bought used from Bergen. This was, by the way, the same type of piano used by Beethoven,

Telemark folk painter Thomas Luraas. In 1930, it served as inspiration for an entire wall of decoration in the hotel dining room. This work was done in cooperation with the well-known Bergen architect, Torgeir Alvsaker, who was born near Utne. He designed many houses in the west country style in the area around the hotel in the 1920's and 1930's.

The guest bedrooms also contain furniture from different times – some of the beds even date to the last century. However, modern comfort has not been sacrificed, for the baths were installed during the last 10–20 years. Utne Hotel is a place where both history and tradition sit deep in the walls and surround the guests from all sides.

300 years of history and tradition

building, which probably dates from the 17th century, is where the district magistrate held court and where the authorities would distinguish between right and wrong. During the 1730's, it is said, costly construction work took place at the guesthouse.

Mother Utne's expansion of the business into a hotel in 1849 is well-documented, with descriptions and photographs. At that time, the main trunk of the hotel under the large pitched roof acquired the size it is today, but with a few changes and additions. Then, both this building and the courthouse were in two stories and in the typical west country style used in guesthouses and large farms at that time – inspired by the houses in Bergen with curved roofs, pairs of small-paned windows on the facade and horizontal wall panels. The courthouse still looks as it did in photographs from the 1860's. The hotel has a large, arched entrance portal on the facade toward the fjord. It sat on a high foundation, and in front was a garden with a barrier wall toward the sea, where small and large boats were drawn up. It has been extended widthwise at the back as well as lengthwise. The fireplace room was once Mother Utne's kitchen, and her extension housed a dining hall, which now is a lounge between the veranda room and the dining room. For a long time, there was a post office in the present reception area, and the guest bedrooms were on the second floor.

In the 1870's, the space in front of the main entrance was extended to make room for a glass veranda with a bedroom above. Around the turn of the century, the roof was modernized with large projections and beam constructions in the gables. At the same time, the roof over the glass veranda was raised to make room for another bedroom in the attic. In 1930, the present dining room was added, with bedrooms and a roof terrace above.

and it is still tuned at the start of each summer season.

The piano is flanked by two high-backed chairs in the Baroque style from around 1700. One of them was found in poor condition in the attic in 1930 and refurbished, while the other is a copy of the old one. Beside the doorway to the dining room is a rather unusual piece of furniture – a console table with the bottom part carved in the same style as the Baroque chairs. The massive lower section was originally the base of a heavy iron stove, and it now has been raised with four thin legs and a tabletop in a much simpler style. In the dining room, the departure point for decoration and shelves on the inner wall was a beautiful 17th-century cupboard in Renaissance style. During the middle of the 19th century, it was rosepainted by the outstanding

Utne Hotel as it stood after Mother Utne's extensive expansion in 1849. The building has typical west coast shape. The original building still stands today, but with additions on both long and short sides, which now, too, are growing old. The outward appearance was changed by the addition of the "Swiss style" roof around 1900. Photograph Knud Knudsen, about 1870, Bergen University Library.

OSE TOURIST HOME
Bygland

With a wood-powered steam boat, hash, and home-baking

At the northern end of Byglandfjord, alongside National Route 39, which runs through Setesdal, is Ose, a cluster of three or four houses and a combined cafeteria and jewelry store. Just by the local grocery store is an exclusive souvenir shop, Ose Ullvare, where the renowned textile artist, Annemor Sundbø, sells beautiful sweaters, jackets, wool blankets, rag rugs and other things. Storstoga, a unique two-and-a-half story notched log building, which Mads Pederssøn had built in 1650, today houses an art gallery. In a new log building right next door is Norway's only

The dining room has been restored to its original blue shades and features simple furniture typical of the period. Traditional Setesdal fare is served here.

During the summer months, the baker woman is at work every day in the hotel basement. Her baked goods often sell out before they have had time to cool (below).

Old musical instruments belong in this environment, where old folk music traditions are still much appreciated.

The lounge is simple but cheerful with un-paneled log walls and furniture from different periods of the 20th century (left).

folk music museum, with a fantastic collection of musical instruments, pictures, and fiddle-making tools.

Ose Tourist Home lies at the heart of this little community. With 14 beds in six different bedrooms, it is not a large or pretentious hotel. Every inch of this lovely yellow wooden building breathes calm, atmosphere, and tradition. The house, which was built in 1909, is thoroughly but carefully restored, both inside and out, and is part of what is known as Ose Cultural Workshop.

An important junction

In the past, Ose was a lively and busy little settlement, with three general stores, a bakery, and two tourist stations. Its location,

The reverently restored building that houses Ose Tourist Home still looks as it did when it was opened in 1909. Across the road is Storstova, with its massive log walls, built in the 1600's.

at the end of Byglandsfjord, made it one of the most important junctions in Setesdal. Back then, it was usual to take the Setesdal Railroad (no longer in service) from Kristiansand to Byglandsfjord. This was the final destination of the railroad, and from here, the steamboats "Bjoren" and "Dølen" went on to Ose. Horse and carriage was the only way to travel further into the valley until the 1920's, when the first buses started running between Ose and Valle. In both instances, it was usual to spend the night at Ose. The settlement was the natural meeting place for locals, traveling Setesdal residents, tourists, and civil servants. The town's two tourist stations gave the guests well-deserved rest on their long journey. Here they could gather strength for the next leg of their trip, eat and drink well, and exchange news and gossip.

A tourist business grows

The first tourist station was established in 1887 on the site where Ose Tourist Home stands today. Aslaug and Såvi Ose owned it, but Christiansand & Opland's Tourist Society backed it and paid the family a fixed yearly sum to have a room with clean linens and a wash stand available to travelers at any time. After a while, the traffic increased and there was a need for more beds, so the family decided to try their hand at tourism.

The new Ose Tourist Home was built in 1909 and looked as it does today. The hotel was handed down from generation to generation until 1970, when it was closed. Then, this traditional wooden building was used only sporadically as a holiday home. After a while, time took its toll on this venerable building, and in 1986, Bygland municipality bought the hotel in order to demolish it. Fortunately, this did not occur, and instead, the municipality collaborated with various other local and national cultural and commercial organizations to renovate the hotel.

Home baking and a wood-burning steamship

On June 20, 1990, after two years of hectic restoration, Ose Tourist Home was reopened. The place is still owned by Bygland municipality, but it is managed by the Ose Cultural Workshop Corporation, which also manages the folk music museum.

It is not just the exterior and interior of the hotel that has been painstakingly restored. Food traditions, too, also are kept alive here. Only real Norwegian food is served, and the tourists appreciate the mountain trout, kompe (potato dumplings), true Setesdal soup made with smoked lamb, hash, and salt meat with gravy.

The local baking woman is no less popular. She works in the stone cellar at Ose Tourist Home every day during the summer season. Each day, about 50 Hardanger lefse, 40 potato cakes, and 50 sheets of cracker-like flat bread are eaten as soon as they come out of the oven!

At Ose, everything is done as properly and traditionally as possible. Everyone was happy to see the newly restored, old wood-burning steamship, "Bjoren," on the water again. Now, tourists once again can come to Ose by boat from Byglandsfjord via the dam at Storestraumen, just as they did in the good old days.

Ose Tourist Home is characterized by its relatively simple, country setting. It was opened in 1909, and since it took in visitors for the night, it was a little larger than most farm buildings in the area. Today, it is important because it is so well preserved. It is also part of an older milieu which is typical for small country centers from the first half of the 20th century. The tourist home has been beautifully restored by the members of Ose Cultural Workshop in collaboration with the regional cultural preservation department. In the restoration, original elements were emphasized, while at the same time, some newer additions were retained.

Ose Tourist Home was built in shapes which were quite popular in its time. It is typical of the "Swiss style" which was declining in popularity by then. The large roof projections are characteristic, with their visible rafters and beams with profiled ends. The horizontal separation of the floors is clearly marked on the facade with imitations of beam ends and ornaments inspired by old half-timbered buildings on the continent. The pronounced vertical format of the windows, even though the height of the stories is less than often was the case at the time, is another typical trait. This style's almost obligatory veranda is in front of the main entrance on the gable wall facing the road.

Inside, the rooms are arranged along one side of a long corridor which is reminiscent of the galleries of earlier times. The lounge still has unpaneled log walls and features simple furniture from different periods of this century. The dining room and kitchen are once again in their original fresh blue colors. The dining room features a large buffet cupboard from the former Granheim Hotel ten kilometers farther up the valley. It dates from around 1900 and represents a local blend of different styles. The carpentry work is indicative of middle class urban furniture at this time, and the painting imitates mahogany and ebony. It is also decorated with carved and gilded acanthus leaves inspired by older folk art, so it represents both urban and rural furniture traditions.

The kitchen is exceptionally well-preserved, with no modern additions. During restoration, it has once again been given a simple, old-fashioned counter with a plate rack above. Under the chimneypiece is an electric stove, but it is a much older model than one usually finds today. The kitchen is painted blue, as in earlier days, when people believed that the color kept the flies at bay.

Simple and honest

Ose quay was an important center of communication in Setesdal until bus traffic took over in 1920. In this valley, folk costumes were in daily use much longer than in other places in Norway. Photograph from around 1910, National Office of Historic Monuments archives.

The guest rooms are decorated with furniture and wall treatments from different periods in this century. One room has been turned into a bath, while the others still have old-fashioned washstands with pitchers and bowls. During restoration, those in charge were far-sighted enough to retain one room in the style of the 1960's. It is decorated with contemporary furniture, and walls are covered in veneer sheets clad with plastic imitation teak. It was a popular wall covering in its time, but today, it is regarded with contempt. Soon it will be rare, but here it will be preserved. The reception area used to be a post office and retains much of its original inventory, also in the style of the 1960's.

Across the road is Storstova, a wonderful building from around 1650. Two-story houses were not at all common in Setesdal in those days, but this one was built for Danish rural magistrate Mads Pederssøn. It was clearly patterned after elegant houses with stairwells far away from the farmhouses of the valley. But the building techniques are in line with valley traditions, with thick notched logs hewn into oval shapes. The house was incomplete at Mads Pederssøn's death. Eventually, it was utilized as a hay barn, with shutters in front of the window openings. Around 1904, Storstova was moved to its present site by a group of religious societies, which used the building as a prayer house and meeting hall. At that time, it was given its present roof and windows, which are higher and smaller than the old ones, traces of which can be seen in the logs. After some repairs in 1990, the building is now used as an art gallery. The peculiar, low doorway is an old Setesdal type and was inserted during restoration.

RAFOSS HOTEL
Kvinesdal

The sheriff's daughters who started a hotel

Liknes is right by European Route 18, 100 kilometers west of Kristiansand. This little village, with a beautiful octagonal wooden church from 1837 as its natural center, is the commercial and administrative center of Kvinesdal municipality. Along Nesgata, the main street, are a row of charming white wooden houses, and Rafoss Hotel, at number 12, is one of the country's most distinctive small hotels.

Its story began in 1908, when Samuel T. Rafoss bought the idyllic lot on the banks of the Kvina, one of Norway's best salmon rivers. He had just become sheriff in the area after his father-in-law, and he wanted to build a suitable home for himself and his family. But Samuel was an industrious and far-sighted man. Why not take advantage of the increasing traffic of English salmon lords who came every year and bought fishing rights on the Kvina from nearby landowners? Samuel built a large home with enough rooms for an inn. In addition, his wife Karoline had her own shop in the fine new building. Both worked hard and earned enough to be considered wealthy. But, unfortunately, neither lived long. Samuel died at age 46 in 1925, and Karoline at age 55 six years later.

The entrance to Rafoss Hotel is influenced by southern Norwegian Classicism.

Old family portraits in the salon give the room a comfortable, homey atmosphere (right).

"The Misses Rafoss' Hotel"

Karoline and Samuel had three children, daughters Agnes and Inga, and son Thorleif. After her mother died, Agnes became responsible for the inn, the shop and her two younger siblings, no small job for a 24-year-old! And on top of it all, there was an accident. The following year, in 1932, a huge fire destroyed the entire row of houses along the Kvina, including their own. But Agnes refused to give up. The children had inherited some money from their parents, so that same year, they built the present hotel on the original lot. Agnes and Inga, three years younger, ran the hotel, which was called "The Misses Rafoss' Hotel" by the locals. Both had "trained" at their parents' knees. The little hotel quickly became a success. An overly enthusiastic magazine reporter wrote about them in the 1930's under the following headline: "Two young ladies run the ideal small hotel: Two very young sisters, Misses Agnes and Inga Rafoss, have built a hotel which is an oasis for travelers. The hotel is a pleasant green color, with black window and door frames. In front of the house is a well-maintained garden, while on the other side of the hotel is a beautiful terrace, which extends all the way to the steep banks of the mighty river. An incomparable view from there! Inside, every detail in color, furnishing and practical arrangements has been thought out by these young ladies. And in every corner there is evidence that they have understood their task."

From Miss to Mrs.

In addition to salmon fishermen, traveling salesmen were the most important customers in those days. The years passed, and The Misses Rafoss' Hotel was soon a landmark in Kvinesdal. Eventually, both married. During the war, Inga married Halvor Skappel, a railroad engineer from Oslo, and she moved to the capital. Agnes was alone at the hotel for a while, but in 1946, she married sea captain Thomas Kaurin Johansen. When their only child, son Bård, was born three years later, he went on land for good, and he and Agnes ran the hotel together. During the 1950's, they modernized somewhat. They raised the attic roof to make new guest bedrooms on the third floor, and they built a new wing onto the main building to make a larger dining room.

A roaring fire welcomes the guests.

This Biedermeier group of furniture can be found in the lounge (left).

The dining room has been newly redecorated in the old style. On the walls are old pictures of King Haakon and Queen Maud.

During the 1960's, the salmon fishermen disappeared from Kvinesdal. Acid rain and waste released into the river from Knaben mines had killed the salmon in the Kvina. As time went on, there were fewer traveling salesmen, but there was an increase in the number of other businessmen who came to the area. The new clientele demanded increased comfort, and in the middle of the 1970's, another wing was added, this time with modern, comfortable bedrooms. One of the first guests in the new wing was the world famous author Roald Dahl, who visited in the summer of 1976.

A new generation takes over

Modernization in stages meant, of course, that the hotel lost much of its original purity of style. When Bård Johansen took over the hotel after his mother, he had a choice between leaving everything as it was or renovating thoroughly. He chose the latter, and with his wife Kari, he began the extensive and laborious task of restoring the hotel. They invested money, time and patience into bringing it back to its pre-war original style. The result was successful, and when the 1995 summer season began, Kari and Bård Johansen could welcome guests to a distinctive hotel filled with nostalgia and the atmosphere of times long gone. The exterior of the hotel is, of course, painted white in the tradition of southern Norway. Inside, the dining room and lounges have been restored to their earlier elegance, with shiny parquet floors, ceiling plasterwork, impressive chandeliers and antique furniture.

Business travelers are still the hotel's main group of customers during the winter, but tourists dominate during the summer. Most Norwegians associate Kvinesdal with the Valley of Sharon and Aril Edvardsen's popular revival meetings, but many have also discovered the natural beauty of this West Agder town. The county is large and the landscape varies from fjord to mountain. On the same day, you can swim in Feda and then climb high up in the mountains to visit the old, shuttered molybdenum mines at

Knaben. In Fjotland, you can participate in an exciting moose and beaver safari, and from Kvinesdal, you can embark on other tours of the district. The distance to Norway's southernmost point, Lindesnes, is not far, and the cozy southern towns, Mandal, Kristiansand and Flekkefjord are not so far away either. In addition, many years of liming in the Kvina have begun to take effect. It is once again possible to fish salmon in the river, and maybe the salmon lords will return to traditional Rafoss Hotel.

Rafoss Hotel looks like a wealthy home in the south of Norway, as it stands in the row of white wooden buildings in the center of Liknes. Its predecessor on the same lot was both an inn and a country store, a two-story building in the style typical of the decades around 1900, with "Swiss style" roof extensions and high windows.

After a fire in 1932, a building with roots in the local traditions was erected. The architect was Gabriel Tallaksen from Kristiansand, and he designed a house in the style which had been used by shipowners and

Other smaller additions followed on the long side by the river and on the one short wall, all featuring the same detailing as the original building.

A new, modern guest wing, designed by architect Halfdan Wendt from Mandal, was added to the old building around 1975. Built with a modern concrete skeleton, the outer facades were covered with light brick. With its low pitched roof, it was much better suited to the original building than the thoughtless contrasts which otherwise were so common at that time.

century. In the lounge and reception area are many family pictures, including good portraits of those who have run the hotel and inn here. They are painted by Marcelius Førland (1891-1978) from Kvinesdal, who is especially known for his landscapes of the region and for his portraits.

Southern Neo-Classicism

other wealthy people in Sørlandet at the end of the 18th and the first half of the 19th centuries. The original style is usually called Sørland Classicism or Sørland Empire and is similar to that of western Norway from the same period.

The simple rectangular floor plan and high curved roof are typical of the style here. In the gables, the apexes are cut off to make what usually is called a half-hipped roof. This kind of roof has long traditions in Denmark and north Germany, where it still can be found in many old houses. It was brought to Norway at the end of the 18th century and often was used by civil servants and other wealthy people throughout the country, but especially in the southern part. It seems that the new hotel building from 1932 established a pattern for many of the neighboring houses in Liknes.

The facade's main element is, as in older models, an entrance portal in typical shapes from around 1800, with flat, columnar pilasters on the side and a hemispherical window above. Because of its rather delicate proportions, this version of Classicism is often called Louis XVI style. Traditionally, the windows consist of many small panes of glass. The exterior was originally painted light green with black trim, a modern influence from the 1930's.

Smaller additions followed. Just after the Second World War, the attic was extended by raising the roof and adding the dormers which exist to this day.

Throughout the years, the interiors have been subjected to both modernization and wear. They were completely renovated in 1995. The parquet floors have been beautifully restored, while the rest of the hotel features new elements in older styles. In the lounge, there is an old sofa in Biedermeier style from around 1840 and an impressive sitting group in Danish Biedermeier Revival from the first years of this

The Rafoss sisters' hotel from 1923 is constructed in pure Sørlandet style. The original colors, pale green walls with black trim, seem unusual today. The hotel was brand new in this photograph and the latest mode of transportation stands outside. Photograph: Private collection.

HOTEL NORGE
Lillesand

Where Knut Hamsun was a regular guest

The charming southern town of Lillesand lies just about halfway between Grimstad and Kristiansand. This town, which was originally called Sanden, is mentioned in the tax book for Denmark/Norway as early as 1610. The first people to settle in Lillesand in the 1600's were seafaring tradesmen. The town grew steadily from these small beginnings to its golden age during the sailing ship era at the end of the 1800's. A its height, the town's shipowners had a total of 78 ships and numerous wharves. Lillesand was then, unlike today, very much a part of the pulsating Europe. Sailing ships from Lillesand sailed on every sea, and sailors brought European culture back with them to the old country. Today, this can best be seen in the town's architecture and building styles. English sliding windows, Dutch roof tiles, and half-hipped roofs are proud reminders of Lillesand's golden age as a powerful shipping town.

A hotel is founded

With its narrow streets, small, cozy white painted houses, and large, handsome mansions, Lillesand is often considered the prettiest town in southern Norway. Strandgate is the town's walking street. Shipowners used to live here, by the sea, in their beautiful, patrician houses. In its days of prosperity as a seafaring town, Lillesand was divided according to income and status. The merchants lived a bit further up in the town, while the skippers and the pilots lived in Øvregate (Upper Street). Even further up in the town, and farthest away from the sea, lived lowly seamen and laborers.

Traditional Hotel Norge – a beautiful white painted building with a much varied history – is on Strandgaten. The hotel's history began with a storybook figure, Irish rebel Robert Gonsalvo Major. Born in Belfast in 1766, he participated in the Irish rebellion of 1798 and fled to Norway in 1799. He settled in Kristiansand as a trader. In 1837, he came to Lillesand, and during the following two years, he constructed both a bark mill and factory buildings for a tannery. In order to run his businesses properly, he needed offices

The renovation has concentrated on using old furniture together with fresh colors and graphic works by Ferdinand Finne.

The dining room is in the old wooden building and has a beautiful view (left).

The lounges are furnished mainly with items from around the turn of the century. On the walls are portraits of Norway's Kings and the Norwegian Coat of Arms.

After restoration and renovation in the 1990's, the old part of Hotel Norge looks just as it did when the two original buildings were connected in 1890 (left).

and a warehouse, so he built what is today the oldest part of Hotel Norge.

But despite his success in business, Major was not a happy man and he committed suicide in 1839. Part of his property was sold to Gunder Carlsen. This shoemaker's son from Lofthus had sailed at sea and taken his navigator exam, when in 1864, he became owner of the land and the house which is part of the hotel today.

However, things did not go so well for Carlsen either, and the place was sold at auction to Anders Eriksen Gitmark in 1868. He owned the property for 22 years, and during this period, people who rented from Gitmark started a hotel in the building. No one knows the identity of these people, but hotel records note that it opened in 1873.

A Dane takes over the hotel

In 1890, Lars Gitmark sold the hotel to Lars Jensen, later nicknamed "Jensen in Norway". Jensen came to Lillesand from Faaborg in Fyn. He had fought as a soldier in the Danish-German war of 1864, he and arrived in Lillesand in the 1870's. He managed Hotel Denmark on Østregate before taking over Hotel Norge in 1890. This was right in the middle of Lillesand's golden age, and the hotel quickly became the center for the town's blossoming cultural life. Jansen constructed a tennis court and a bowling alley outside the hotel, and inside, he equipped both a billiard table and a theater. Despite this, the hotel did not always do well and money was tight. World War I brought food shortages, rationing, and high inflation to Lillesand.

Famous guests

After a while, Jensen sold the hotel to shipmaster Peder Christian Lindeberg and his wife. Knut Hamsum, the famous Norwegian author, was a regular customer during their time. It has often been claimed that he wrote some of his books here, but this is uncertain. It is known that Hamsun often visited Hotel Norge during the first half of the 1930's, and that Lindeberg made sure that

Knut Hamsun often visited Hotel Norge. He always stayed in this room, and today it bears the famous author's name.

he always got the same room. Today, that room bears Hamsn's name. If the author did indeed write something during his many stays at Hotel Norge, it is reasonable to assume that it was part of his trilogy of novels published between 1927 and 1933.

Another famous guest visited the hotel at this time. In 1931, the year he abdicated, King Alphonso XIII of Spain set sail on a cruise to Norway. He traveled incognito as the Duke of Toledo. One day, he anchored in Lillesand and checked into Hotel Norge. He must have been enthusiastic about the place, his room and the view, because he scratched the words Alfons Rex into the mirror with his diamond ring.

Under Mrs. Lindeberg's leadership, the kitchen at Hotel Norge became widely known for its delicious

food. Perhaps this was the reason that the couple decided to sell the hotel and move to Grimstad, where they ran a boarding house during the summer and Mrs. Lindeberg ran a home economics school during the winter.

Hotel Norway today

After the Lindeberg's left, Hotel Norge went into a long period of changing economic conditions and different owners. There was Mrs. Tangvall, Mrs. Holmen, Jenny Strøm, Sverre Langfeldt, and Mossa Foss. Of all these, only the last two left any traces on the hotel. Sverre Langfeldt undertook a thorough restoration, which was absolutely necessary after long years of war and occupation.

Miss Mossa Foss from Geilo expanded the hotel, and with her excellent taste and eye for details, made it an inviting and popular gathering place. Under the leadership of Miss Foss, the hotel experienced its true heyday and she became a legend at Hotel Norge.

Today, Torill Kjær Taranger and her husband, Nils Arne, own and manage this traditional southern hotel. They took it over in 1992 from Arnt T. Johansen and his wife, who had run it since 1984. From 1992 to 1995, the Tarangers thoroughly restored the hotel. The result is a modern and comfortable hotel, where culture and history have been preserved in its old buildings. Hotel Norge is still one of gems on the idyllic southern coast.

Hotel Norge's large wooden building did not begin as a hotel at all. At first, it consisted of two smaller buildings at angles to one another. They were built in 1837-1838 by the immigrant Irishman Robert Gonsalvo Major to house a tannery, office, general store and warehouse. In the back were large basins for tanning and a water mill for the bark which was used in the tanning process.

The first hotel there was opened in 1873, but larger construction work is not known before a Dane, Lars Jensen, took over in 1890. He built the two older

modernized gradually, in many steps, both inside and out, so that it lost its original character. It was re-opened in 1994 after comprehensive restoration overseen by Ragnhild and Thore Drange, from the architectural firm Drange and Aanensen in Arendal. This work has involved reconstructing the exterior of the wooden building to its 1890 state and reproducing the original decor which had been removed along the way. The veranda gallery over the main entrance toward the east was reproduced, with red and blue glass as the outer wall in one of the lounges on the second floor. The guest bedrooms in

roof beams on the upper floor reveal the old building materials. The dining room is furnished in the old style, while the lounges are decorated with antiques acquired in the last few years. In this way, the interiors have a nostalgic atmosphere created by combining both old and new elements.

In 1985, the hotel took over a smaller house now furnished as a pub. This building was erected in 1864 with a restrained decor and a hint of the "Swiss style" in the roof projections. It retains its original shape, but the furnishings inside are new.

Gothic Revival and nostalgia

structures into the wooden building which still serves as the main part of the hotel. It also housed a billiard parlor, theater and outdoor bowling alley. When it was renovated, the hotel acquired large projecting roofs with visible rafters and ridges in the "Swiss style." The decoration on the gable and in the open veranda gallery on the east side shows the influence of the Gothic Revival, which was very popular at the time. The specific shapes used here were fashionable in the Lillesand and Grimstad area, created by architect Frederik von der Lippe at the end of the 1860's for the house he designed at Snøringsmoen in Lillesand for shipowner and timber merchant Lars Hammer Jr. This house still looks out over the town and is presently (1996) being carefully restored after a fire. It is owned by Lillesand's tireless advocate of historic building conservation, Else Rønnevig, who runs a cultural and historical restaurant-hotel in the house.

Hotel Norge was extended with a new concrete guest wing in the 1960's. The rest of the hotel was

the 1960's wing were equipped with large glass bay windows on the courtyard side. Inside, the dining room, with its small salon, and in the lounges were refurbished in the old style, and some reproduction wallpaper has been used. The irregularities in the

Hotel Norge after reconstruction during the 1890's. After modernizations over many years, the exterior once again has been restored as it was 100 years age. In this photograph, the son of the host is welcoming his new fiancée around 1895. Photograph lent from Helge's studio, Lillesand.

Hotel Norge has been Lillesand's grand hotel since the turn of the century. After a long and varied history, it is now a modern hotel with most conveniences, but in the exterior and in some of the furnishings inside, the atmosphere of a bygone era has been recreated.

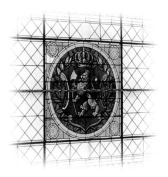

HOTEL DALEN
Dalen

At the last station on the Telemark Canal

"Hotel Dalen. The new, elegantly furnished hotel at Dalen is now ready to receive visitors. The Management".

This advertisement appeared in Varden newspaper on July 17, 1894. Finally, the tiny, beautiful settlement of Dalen, one of Norway's largest tourist centers at the turn of the century, had the large hotel it so badly needed.

The building of the road brought tourists to Dalen. The village was an important crossroads – the routes from Hardanger, Roga-land, Agder, Kragerø, Skien, Kongsberg and Tinn all converged here. The beautiful Telemark countryside, with high and mighty mountains, steep and narrow valleys, and lush green lowlands all attracted tourists. But art and culture were also important. Many of our popular and beloved fairy tales, legends and folk songs originated in Telemark. This, along with all the beautiful old farms, storehouses and stave churches, as well as the fact that Telemark has always been the "capital" of rosepainting, made Dalen a popular destination for tourists from home and abroad.

The canal laid the foundation

After the Telemark Canal opened in 1892, tourist traffic to Dalen increased dramatically. There was a direct boat between Skien and Dalen, and from Skien, there were steamships to England, Germany and France. In addition, there was scheduled boat traffic from Dalen to Oslo, or Christiania, as it was called in those days, with a connection at Skien. From the very beginning, the canal was a major tourist attraction. People came to experience the fantastic boatride, and there was a flood of tourists to Telemark. In July, 1893, 4000 people visited the tiny village of Dalen, the same number that usually visited in an entire year.

Because of this development, a group of wealthy men from Skien decided to build a large and exclusive hotel in the village. Because "...when the fast boat arrived at around 11 p.m., there was nowhere near enough lodging for all, so that many had to stay in less comfortable accommodation nearby or stay on board in the smokers' lounge or any other place on the steamship; many had to put up with a chair on a hotel veranda or even sleep under the stars."

The guest bedrooms have been newly renovated in the old style. Some of the rooms are decorated with pieces of old furniture.

Thanks to comprehensive repairs, this fantastic wooden building stands today as it has done for over a hundred years (right).

The main hall stands today much as it did when it was built. It features national romantic elements combined with medieval-inspired carving. The entire ceiling is a large glass painting with the Norwegian coat of arms as the central motif.

the first guests came in July. According to the standards of the day, the hotel was both lavish and luxurious. It even had running water and electric lights. It was no wonder that Hotel Dalen was a success from the start! It attracted elegant people from all of Europe. King Leopold II of Belgium visited in 1904, and in 1912, King Haakon, Queen Maud and little Prince Olav spent the night there. Other guests included the King of Siam, King Oscar II and Kaiser Wilhelm of Germany.

Business was good until the First World War. Then, there were fewer tourists all over Europe, and even though Norway was neutral, business still tapered off. Hotel Dalen had major losses and had to reorganize in 1918, with a new subscription of shares. The Travel Association took over the shares, and the share capital was expanded to 125,000 crowns. From 1935 to 1938, the hotel was modernized and 11 rooms got private baths.

Those were the conditions in Dalen in 1893. Something had to be done about that. A big hotel was needed! An interest group was established, and a general meeting was held on December 4, 1893. This was a completely private enterprise, and the chairman was Hans Larsen from Skien, who already owned the Grand Hotel there. He was also one of the founders of the newspaper "Varden" and later became mayor of Skien. With him were wholesaler Lars Rød, also from Skien, and merchant Anthon Hansen from Porsgrunn.

A hotel with fashionable clientele

The new hotel was officially opened on September 8, 1894, but

War and decline

Then came the Second World War. Life went on pretty much as before during the first three years of the war, but on September 29, 1943, German soldiers took over the beautiful building. From then on, it was used to house Polish prisoners of war. During that period, the hotel was stripped of much of its earlier beauty, and some parts were severely damaged.

After the war ended, a real estate agent from Oslo, Bjarne Bjørndalen bought the hotel and renovated it. He and his family ran it during the 1940's and 1950's. At that time, many Danish tourists came to Dalen by bus. Bjørndalen hired help to run the

The hotel lounges feature some old furniture suites. Unfortunately, most of the original furniture has disappeared over the years. In the hall, the original wallpaper, an imitation of gilded leather, still can be seen above the Renaissance Revival style wainscoting.

business during the last years before the hotel was sold at forced auction for 350,000 crowns in 1966.

Tore Berdal, who took over the hotel, also used hired management. There were a number of years with many different managers, until Oskar Dalen bought the hotel on behalf of the Dalen Tourist Foundation in 1974. The foundation was backed by the Norwegian Mission Federation, who managed the hotel until it was closed by the health authorities in 1982. The owners did not have enough money to pay off their bank loan, nor to keep the hotel running, and they certainly did not have any for remodeling. There was no other option than to let the hotel be sold at a forced auction. The National Office of Historic Monuments noted that the hotel was especially worthy of preservation, but there was no money on the budget for restoration. Uncertain times followed, and the once so honorable wooden building was put up for sale for 600,000 crowns.

The Women's University or God's will

In 1983, associate professor Berit Ås wanted the building for the Women's University, where women of all ages and backgrounds and from different countries could receive educations. Those behind this project were so certain that they would be able to buy it that they began fixing it up. Then the evangelist Aage Samuelsen swept in. God had told him to buy the "wreck," as the hotel was called locally, and he bid 750,000 crowns. "A Women's University will only shame Telemark," he maintained. He himself had plans to restore the hotel back to its original style and open the doors to everyone.

"Brother Aage uses God's help against women," wrote a Swedish paper. Whether due to God's help or not, Aage Samuelsen had the winning bid, but it was up to the municipality to give him a license. Berit Ås would not give up until this problem was solved, and there was lively debate in the press. Meanwhile, in 1985, the deed to the hotel was transferred to Aage Samuelsen and Dalen Revival, Inc. Unfortunately, not even Aage and his friends could finance the restoration, and on July 7, 1987, the hotel once again was on its way to a forced sale.

The hotel stood empty until the 100th anniversary of the Telemark Canal in 1992, when the corporate owners, Hotel Dalen,

Inc., with the municipality the major shareholder, could welcome guests to a newly restored hotel. The beautiful hotel was fixed up completely and the present exterior is almost exactly as it was on its opening day in 1894. From 1996, the management of the hotel has been leased to the Viking Hotel chain, who promise that guests will be able to enjoy genuine, historical atmosphere at one of Norway's most famous hotels well into the future.

With its 82 meter long facade facing Bandak Lake, Hotel Dalen is not just one of the really large tourist hotels from the time around the turn of the century; today, it is also one of the best preserved. After extensive restoration work in cooperation with the National Office of Historic Monuments, the hotel has regained its original splendor after many years of decline. Inside, the most important interiors are well preserved. The standard of the guest bedrooms has risen considerably, while the original style and ambiance have

A palace with dragon style shapes

been preserved to a great degree in the furnishings and decor.

Porsgrunn architect Haldor Børve (1857-1933) designed the new construction. He was educated in Hannover at the end of the 1880's, and thus was greatly influenced by that era's German wooden architecture in fundamental shapes and verandas. Roof ridges and gable apexes are decorated with Norwegian dragon shapes taken from our old stave churches. The long body of the building is broken on both long sides by perpendicular wings which have varying roof heights, gables and verandas to break up the long lines and to avoid monotony. The richest formulations are concentrated in the central section with two towers placed in pairs on each main facade. On the courtyard side, the rising lines in the inner staircases are used to give the facades extra life with slanted windowbands. The midsection is crowned with a larger construction which both protects and lets light in to the large glass painting in the ceiling over the central hall. The result is a completely unusual building, which, in spite of its strict symmetry, still gives the impression of an airy and fantastic combination of different shapes and constructions.

The interiors live up to the richness promised by the exterior. The entrance leads to the great two-story central hall. This is the communication center of the house, with doors to lounges by the water and to the corridors with guest bedrooms out in the long wings. On one side is the kitchen and food preparation area, with the dining room in its own wing. The hall under the great glass roof has rich carpentry

work. Some larger arched openings allow the evening light in from the west. Under the ceiling cornice is an arched frieze supported by small Romanesque style columns. The sources of inspiration here were the galleries in stave churches and in Norwegian storehouses from the Middle Ages. Influence from stave churches is also clear in the diagonal crosses or so-called St. Andrew's crosses, which are used in the wall panels facing the hall on the second floor. The high wainscoting at the bottom of the walls also features a richly carved arched frieze, but in a manner typical for the Renaissance of the 1600's. Otherwise, the walls are papered with an imitation of gilt leather dating from the time the hotel was built. A large fireplace open on two sides is a unifying element in the large room. This hall is inspired by those in medieval castles and by contemporary villas and hotels in other parts of Europe.

The hotel always had its three lounges facing the garden. Alongside the large lounge in the center were separate lounges for men and women. All have richly decorated ceilings divided into paneled sections painted in many different color nuances, with stenciled decor in the center sections. The southern lounge features rich decorative painting on the walls with an illusion of wainscoting with walls painted in stripes and garlands. The entire hotel is quite typical of interior decoration in the 1890's. This is emphasized by the lace curtains and by the furniture, some of which is in the Renaissance Revival style from the

same period. Unfortunately, the original furniture has not been preserved. The older furniture which is now in use was bought in conjunction with the most recent renovations and there are plans to purchase more.

The dining room also is richly decorated with wainscoting and a ceiling divided into sections. The walls feature diagonal panels. The buffet niches serve as focal points on either side of the Renaissance Revival main entrance. As everywhere else at the hotel, grand proportions are the order of the day. A unifying theme in the common rooms at Hotel Dalen is the treatment of the woodwork. For the most part, it remains as it was when the hotel was opened, with brown, oiled surfaces, with the pattern of the wood quite evident, typical of the time.

From the beginning, Hotel Dalen was a strange place. It still stands as it was built in 1894. Photograph: Knud Knudsen, about 1900, National Office of Historic Monuments archives.

When the hotel was restored around 1990, all guest rooms were given private baths. In order to comply with fire protection laws, and because of additional insulation, water mains and ventilation ducts, the walls and ceilings had to be renewed. Simple panels, similar to the original, were used, while the old doors and windows in the guest rooms have been retained wherever possible. Panels and doors have been painted in a large number of color nuances, as was usual in the 1890's.

Hotel Dalen has avoided being overpowered by new and large extensions. And the richly detailed lounges have not been subjected to thorough remodeling according to changing tastes and trends. Any remodeling, refurbishing or even purchase of new furniture has taken into account the style of the hotel as it was built. For this reason, it is still possible to experience a grand hotel as it was during the "Belle Époque" of the tourist hotel before World War I, here at Hotel Dalen.

NUTHEIM GUESTHOUSE
Flatdal

An artists' hotel in Telemark

Nutheim guesthouse lies in Flatdal, in the upper part of Telemark, just between Hjartdal and Seljord. National Route 11 winds past, right outside the house wall and makes this traditional hotel a charming stopping place. The beautiful white-painted building stands tall and free, with a fantastic view of both mountains and valleys. At the front of the house is a lovely, large garden, and behind the hotel looms majestic Bindingsnuten, the mountain which gave the hotel its name.

During the 1860's, when the road from Seljord was rerouted eastward to Notodden and Kongsberg, the foundation for the hotel business at Nutheim was laid. The crossroads at Svingen, by the exit to Åmotsdal, was an ideal place. The hotel was finished in 1877, and outwardly, little has changed since then. It has been in continuous operation since it was opened.

Frequent changes of ownership
Nutheim was constantly changing owners during its first 40 years of operations. General store owner O.A. Olsen founded it, combining a general store, entertainment, refreshments, and beds for the night. After he died, his widow sold the business to Halvor Romnes for 6000 crowns.

Romnes was a good businessman, and he ran the place successfully until 1899, when he sold it to bank cashier L. Gisholt, wholesaler Hans Andersen, merchant P.B. Pedersen and traveling salesman A.C. Anderud. Within a year, they sold the business to Johannes Almankås, who did not last long at Nutheim, either. In 1901, the property was sold at auction for 13,653.97 crowns to widow Gina Thommesen, who had great plans for the hotel. She planted the beautiful garden, with its lilac bushes, birch trees, gravel paths, and duck pond. Unfortunately, Gina's stay at Nutheim was not long, either. After she died in 1904, her foster son, Ove Pihlfeldt, from Kragerø, inherited the hotel. He moved to Nutheim but stayed only two years before selling it to Halvor S. Haugstoga.

The lounges in the main building of the guesthouse are filled with rustic antiques and 20th-century art.

Bindingsnuten, the mountain which gave the hotel its name, looms in the background (right).

For the first two years, Halvor rented the hotel to Anne Hjartsjø, who was educated at the Boulevard Hotel and Catering School, and who had been the chef at the Business Association in Christiania. She was an excellent hostess, but after only two years at Nutheim, she married and decided to liquidate the business. Now, Halvor took over the hotel, but he sold it in 1913 to Gunleik H. Mæland for 16,000 crowns. For Gunleik, this was an excellent buy. The First World War was entering its second half, and the prices of property and merchandise were soaring. When Gunleik sold Nutheim in 1917 to brothers Olav and Harald Svartdal, the price tag was 36,000 crowns.

A family-run artists' hotel

Nutheim Guesthouse entered a new epoch with the Svartdal brothers. Since then, it has been run by the same family. In the early 1920's, the brothers married two sisters, Gunhild and Bergit Nes from Seljord. Gunhild and Olav ran both the guesthouse and the farm which had always belonged to it, and Bergit and Harald managed the general store. The guest house prospered under Gunhild and Olav's excellent leadership, and as early as 1926, they felt the need to expand. The hotel was especially popular among the country's artists. One by one, they came to Nutheim, led by Erik Werenskiold, Erik Sørensen, Harald Kihle, and Kai Fjell. They came first and foremost to get inspiration from the beautiful Telemark landscape. Flatdal is special because of its many valleys, which provide excellent subjects for landscape painters. And Bindingsnuten mountain, with its listed and protected buildings, has always been a favorite motif for artists. Year after year, they returned, and their love for the area is probably best expressed by the following quote from Henrik Sørensen's eulogy after the death of Werenskiold in 1939, "They will ask for him, of course, the bear and the fox, close to the autumn hills now, the snow is expected. The princess and the boy will go out into the castle hallway and look and listen for him. The forest and the mountain will plaintively ask for their redeemer."

Many artists came to this "artists' hotel" during the Second World War, including Rudolph Thygesen, Sigurd Winge, Kaare Espolin Johnson, Arne Kavli, Ridley Borchgrevink, Harald Dal, and Willy Middelfart. At Nutheim, they could work in peace and quiet in pleasant surroundings, and here they created works which live on in the history of Norwegian art.

This bed in one of the guest rooms in the old parsonage is a museum piece from Tinn in Telemark. It features elements from several different stylistic periods, as is often the case with rustic art. The swollen shapes come from 18th century Baroque, while the two portrait medallions of King Oscar I and Queen Josephine place the bed in the middle of the 19th century.

This guest room in the old parsonage has old canopy beds which have been restored by Erlend Grøstad.

Hotel and school of art

Today Nutheim is run by artist Erlend Grøstad and his wife Anne. Anne, called Ninni by friends and guests alike, is the daughter of Gunhild and Olav, and the couple took over the hotel from her parents in 1957. Their daughter, sculptor Ellen Grøstad Barstad, also helps to run the place.

With such an artistic host family, it is only natural that artistic traditions live on at Nutheim. From May to September, Erlend Grøstad arranges painting and drawing courses at the guesthouse. Each course lasts a week, and is based on ideas created by the Norwegian students of Matisse and painters of the Telemark school. The instruction examines the development from sketch to finished painting, and there are courses for beginners, amateurs, and advanced artists. At the courses, which are arranged in cooperation with the open university, students learn to develop their visual capabilities in an artistic direction.

The furnishings in the main dining room are new, but influenced by old country traditions and styles.

The old parsonage

But Erlend Grøstad is not just a painter and host. He calls himself a culture broker. In 1962, he bought venerable Holm Parsonage in Hjartdal, which is several hundred years old. He wanted to make an example of how to preserve and restore old houses to today's standards. To do this, he tore down the vicarage and moved it eight kilometers down the valley and rebuilt it at Nutheim. Today this lovely log building serves as part of this traditional artists' hotel.

Nutheim Guesthouse is not a large hotel. There are seven guest bedrooms in the old main building, and six in the parsonage. The guesthouse is run in the traditional way. The peaceful, cozy atmosphere pervades everything and everyone. Of course, the food is traditional, too, as it should be in an artists' hotel, where both father and daughter are artists, and the beautiful lounges are filled with original paintings and bronze sculptures. In addition, the hotel has its own art gallery. At Nutheim, both art and hospitality still are top priority.

Telemark building traditions influenced the style of hotel erected at Nutheim in 1877. The same building still stands today, but with minor extensions at the east end dating from 1926 and 1982. With two stories and a simple rectangular floor plan, it was hardly different from new farmhouses on larger farms in the district at the time. That was also true of the exterior, with its typical vertical wood panels with narrow, profiled lintels, typical among well-off cityfolk in southern Norway. The relatively long roof projections show the influence of the "Swiss style," but the roof angle is the same as that used in Telemark's traditional turf roofs. The roof projections were paneled on the underside and give the impression of being as thick as a turf roof. The original window frames also bore influence of the "Swiss style" but have since been simplified. A small version of that time's almost obligatory "Swiss style" veranda was later removed. In its place is the main

This photograph from around 1900 shows how Nutheim probably looked when the building was first constructed in 1877. At that time, there was a shop in one end of the house, and it had a small veranda facing the view. The cariole, a light two-wheel carriage drawn by a single horse, was the most common vehicle on Norwegian country roads before the automobile took over. Photograph: Private collection.

Clean lines and colorful art

entrance in a projection on the long wall, built in the same style as the rest of the building.

Inside, the building has been changed considerably through the years. For a time, there was a general store at the western end, where a lounge is now. The fireplace room used to be the kitchen. It was first moved in 1945 and finally came to its present place at the eastern end of the house in 1982. The dining room also was remodeled in 1982, and the walls are covered with panels with rounded moldings copied from the original panels in the house. The common rooms feature some rustic antiques, including typical Telemark log chairs decorated with the district's typical rosepainting.

The interior features paintings by 20th-century Norwegian artists everywhere. These are primarily in the figurative tradition of Telemark painters and in the colorist style of the Norwegians pupils of Matisse. Of course, there are many works by the innkeeper,

Erlend Grøstad, and some sculptures by his daughter, Ellen. The subjects are mostly landscapes and old buildings in the district, as well as many portraits. Many pictures were gifts to Anne Grøstad's parents, but most have been collected by Anne and Erlend Grøstad.

To conform with fire regulations, the guest bedrooms on the second floor were remodeled. For the most part, traditional moldings have been used, and much consideration has been given to color. All guestrooms have new baths. The furniture is new, but in traditional shapes and in heavy pine. Each room is distinctive because of the paintings by different artists with ties to the place.

Erlend Grøstad has assembled older buildings from the district in a grouping below the guesthouse. The main building here used to be the farmhouse at Holm parsonage in Hjartdal, which may date from the 17th century. The furnishings include old doors

from other houses and beautiful built-in beds and many antiques. An important goal in this restoration has been to show how such an old house can be refurbished to conform to today's demands for comfort without destroying old fixtures and original structures, and without using modern solutions and modern materials. There is a chapel in the cellar, and the building is otherwise decorated with Grøstad's paintings with motifs from the history of the parsonage and with new portraits of its former residents. This grouping includes a new building for Grøstad's school of art, in addition to two old storehouses and Grøstad's own studio in an old log haybarn.

Nutheim has much more to offer than its beautiful view. It is a good place to study the building traditions of West Telemark and at the same time to be surrounded by a rich collection of many artists' interpretations of the landscape and its culture.

TUDDAL MOUNTAIN HOTEL
Tuddal

On the sunny side of Gaustatoppen

As early as the end of the 1880's, people from Sauland and Tuddal began thinking about building a combination sanitarium and tourist hotel in the heart of Telemark. In 1888, members of the Skien-Thelemark Tourist Association evaluated potential sites, and in the spring of 1889, invitations to potential shareholders in the planned establishment were sent. 20,000 crowns were needed, and those taking initiative were farmer and church singer Sv. Bøen from Tuddal, sheriff Kleppen, district physician Paulsson from Sauland, and local parson P. Heiberg Lexow. Unfortunately, no one was interested in investing in the project, so the plans were tabled.It did not take long before new plans were made, this time with attorney Emil Roll taking the initiative.

Emil Roll was born in 1864. After a stay in Romsdal, he returned to Christiania in 1889, where he worked first as a law clerk and later as a lawyer. He was one of the country's first ski enthusiasts, and as head of the Organization to Promote the Sport of Skiing, he established the Holmenkollen medal. Roll was one of many who put city life behind them and went to live in the mountains around the turn of the century. He knew Telemark well, but one day, when he was on his way over the mountain from Tinn, he was completely mesmerized by the view over beautiful Kovstulheia. He had no doubt. Here – surrounded by glittering mountain lakes, scattered evergreen forests and majestic mountains – he would build his sanitarium!

At that time, people were convinced that clean, fresh air at a certain height above sea level was the best remedy for tuberculosis. Kovstulheia, at 850 meters above sea level, had to be perfect for this purpose!

On his way down, he encountered Parson Heiberg Lexow and told him of his plans. The latter was very interested. He had not been scared by the earlier failed endeavor, and he joined with Roll to start the project once again.

Early beginnings
In 1892, Roll and Heiberg Lexow bought three mountain dairy farms with nine buildings at Kovstulheia and in addition, more than 1000 acres of mountain terrain. This time, everything was planned more precisely and more realistically, and in March, 1893, they could offer shares in a "Sanitarium at Kovstulheia."

The amount of capital needed was 100,000 crowns. It was not just a matter of building a hotel with 25 guest bedrooms high in the mountains and without any roads. First, more than five kilometers of road had to be constructed to the center of Tuddal, and then a telephone line had to be laid to the nearest exchange, in Sauland, 27 kilometers away.

For that reason, it was not easy to find investors this time, either. But they were tempted by the prospect of being able to accommodate guests for seven months of the year, and finally the sale of shares was begun. On March 2, 1894, Tuddal's Mountain Sanitarium Company was a fact. Even though the 60,000 crowns minimum share capital had not been raised, there was still optimism that this would work itself out in a couple of years. The company had 82 shareholders, many of whom were local farmers and businessmen. The lawyer and the parson had six shares each. Most shareholders, however, were well-off Christiania gentry, and the owner of the largest number of shares was Conrad Langaard, owner of a tobacco factory. Among other well-known names on the list of shareholders was Gunnar Knudsen, who later became prime minister.

Even the corridors at Tuddal Mountain Hotel are an experience.

The reception area leads to two staircases that curve their way up to the second floor. The hotel has a large collection of Telemark log chairs.
We came here for Christmas and the entire hotel was decorated for the season (following pages).

The dining room has rounded log walls and is filled with antiques, as is the rest of the hotel. Note the plate rack which once hung at the Porsgrunn Porcelain store on Karl Johans gate (the main street) in Oslo.

Constant construction

Construction was started, and on July 15, 1894, the sanitarium could welcome its first guests.

The building of the road, which had been halted for two weeks in May because of a snowstorm, was finally finished. That should have served as a warning, for communication problems hampered running the place for many years.

The telephone lines were finished and functioning. Construction on the main building was in the early stages, but a tourist cabin, a storehouse with five bedrooms and a mountain hut were ready. There was even a fish hatchery. Twelve cows were bought and the services of a milkmaid and a goatherd were hired. It was supposed to produce all its own milk, meat and fish. Mathilde Pettersen, an economist from Buskerud District Hospital, who had worked in Scotland, was hired to manage the place.

The first season was not an unqualified success. Rain and constant construction scared away guests. There was a profit, however, of 429.17 crowns, but almost half of this came from the dairy. The owners persevered. A stable and a bakery were built, and on June 15, 1895, the main building was ready. Even though Roll maintained that Tuddal was the most fashionable sanitarium of the year, that season also was a fiasco. It rained almost continuously for two months, and the result was a profit of 200 crowns.

Two good seasons followed. The number of guests increased, and another cabin with additional beds was built, along with an ice house, slaughterhouse and office building. Tuddal Mountain Sanitarium was its own little village, and in 1897, it even got its own post office.

Forced sales and new companies

But luck turned again. Few off-season guests meant that the slight profits soon turned to stinging losses. Until this time, Tuddal had been open year-round, but now the board decided it should be open during the summer. It was not easy to get to the hotel on the make-shift roads during the winter. In summer, it was simpler. There were enough guests from the middle of July to the middle of August. In fact, sometimes people were turned away. For that reason, Roll wanted to expand the main building, but the investors were not interested. He had many other ideas of how he could make the sanitarium more attractive. Because there was no permanent doctor on the premises, visitors were mostly tourists. He could, of course, hire a doctor, but in order to receive guests coming for recuperation, he would have to build a new rooming house connected to the main building. With such a precarious financial situation, he could just forget that. Another idea was to continue construction of the road over the mountain to Rjukan. This would also have increased the number of travelers, but the other shareholders were not interested. The downswing continued, and in 1902, the sanitarium was forcibly sold for 50,000 crowns, and a new corporation with nine shareholders was formed. The original initiators were still in the picture, while the others were solid farmers from the district. Apart from the change in name, to A/S Tuddal Sanitarium, this reorganization did not involve any significant changes in management. Even though tracts of land were sold every so often, the losses continued. In 1906, the general assembly decided to lease out management of the place. That did not help either, and in 1910, it was put up for sale. It was not easy to find a buyer, and ever the optimist, Roll took over the sanitarium with its buildings, furnishings and five shares in the East Telemark Automobile Company for 43,000 crowns. He called the new corporation A/S Tuddal Mountain Hotel, and he kept nine out of ten shares for himself. His lawyer colleague, I.M. Johannesen, owned the last share.

Of course, Emil Roll could have earned more money by concentrating on his law practice in the capital than by fighting a constant uphill battle at Kovstulheia. But he loved the place and he refused to give up. He had a vision that when he finally succeeded, it would also mean better economic times for the people of Tuddal. But in spite of Roll's undying faith in the project, constant name changes and new corporations, his life work was never a success. He fought alone against creditors, the weather and communications (or lack of), and the stress was just too great. Emil Roll died on September 1, 1934, and a 40-year epoch in the history of the hotel was over.

New owners

In June, 1935, there was another forced sale. The Central Bank for Norway was the purchaser, but the hotel was sold immediately to a corporation called A/S Tuddal for 80,000 crowns. Four people from Oslo sat on the board, chairman Olaf Bjercke, Queen Sonja's father, Karl August Haraldsen, Zakæus Gurholt and Magnhild Simonsen.

Magnhild Simonsen managed the hotel during the first few years and modernized the old main building. Hot and cold water was installed, with sinks in every room, as well as a bathtub on each floor. Toilets were installed in the corridors. All this made work much easier for the chambermaids, who had to run around to all the rooms with jugs of warm water and return with buckets

which had to be emptied of all sorts of things. Finally, in 1938, a generator was installed to supply the main building with electricity. This meant that 35 paraffin lamps no longer had to be polished and filled each day. Electric lights also eliminated the need for candles in the rooms, thus the danger of fire was reduced.

When the Second World War began in April, 1940, tourists fled the hotel in panic. The Germans came and demanded bunk beds in all rooms. Work on the power line from Rjukan to Herøya was begun and it was important to have room for as many workers as possible. Magnhild Simonsen was not interested in running this kind of hotel, so she sold her shares to Zakæus Gurholt and his wife Gudrun.

War and closure

Up to this time, Zakæus, a stock broker and real estate agent in Oslo, had not been involved with the daily management of the hotel. But now he and his wife moved to the mountain. Gudrun had managed a complex of banquet rooms in Oslo, but when the Germans confiscated the locale, she took her large collection of

The current hosts at this traditional hotel are Else and Rune Gurholt Pedersen.

The exterior is well preserved, with some smaller, newer buildings at the far end.

period furniture and placed it in the lounges of the hotel. Mrs. Gurholt was both an enthusiastic collector and a great shopper. Through the years, she added to her collection, and today, few hotels have antiques – furniture, textiles, and decorative objects – which can compare to those at Tuddal Mountain Hotel today.

When peace came in 1945, Zakæus Gurholt was arrested. He had been on the side of the Germans and he had to serve a prison sentence. The Compensation Office took over the hotel, and for a short time, it was used by the Red Cross and called Tuddal Mountain Hotel, Norwegian Red Cross Convalescent Home. Newly-released prisoners of war, who were broken both physically and mentally, came here to regain their strength. After that, the Norwegian home forces took over the hotel for a short period of time and invited their Danish colleagues for a free stay in the mountains.

In 1948, Gurholt returned. He was not satisfied with things as they were. There were barely enough funds to maintain the buildings, so he could not think of modernizing. Luckily, he did not have the expenses of the generator, since Tuddal was electrified just after the war. Eventually, the Telegraph Company took over the private telephone, and the municipality took over responsibility for the road up from Tuddal. Still, there was a downswing. Vacationers demanded higher standards than those offered at Tuddal. In addition, neither Gudrun nor Zakæus was getting any younger, and in the summer of 1967, Zakæus died.

Gudrun continued to run the hotel alone, but it was not easy to breathe life into the old establishment. When Gudrun Gurholt died in 1976, the hotel's days of glory were definitively over.

Tuddal Mountain Hotel today

After Gudrun died, her grandchild, Rune Gurholt Pedersen and his wife Elsa (nee Holst) took over the place. For many years they rented it to a Danish foundation, but in 1993, Elsa and Rune gave notice. They wanted to run the place for themselves. They took down antiques, furniture and knickknacks from the attic. Everything which had been stored since Gudrun died was now put on display. Baths and toilets were installed in the rooms to satisfy modern demands for comfort, but otherwise the hotel is run in the traditional manner. This means personal service, authentic surroundings and good Norwegian food. Many guests come just to enjoy a delicious meal made with local products, but more and more come to the mountains for a longer stay. The hotel is open year-round. During the winter, enthusiastic skiers who want to enjoy snow-clad Telemark fill the hotel, while in the summer, Tuddal Mountain Hotel is an ideal starting point for hikes in the mountain and exploring the district by car. Buen Cultural Workshop, in the center of Tuddal, arranges concerts all summer. Nearby is an open air museum with a collection of old houses and antiques from Telemark. Today, there finally is a road to Rjukan, a popular destination for hotel guests. But still, Gaustatoppen (mountain), 1883 meters high, is still the main attraction. The view from the top covers 1/6 of Norway, and it can be reached from the hotel on skis in the winter, and on foot from the mountain road in the summer. Nature's wonders can be experienced here, where the air is just as fresh and clean as it was in attorney Roll's time, here on the sunny side of Gaustatoppen!

At Tuddal Mountain Hotel, national romantic architecture is the order of the day, with its brown, unpaneled walls of planed notched logs. On the roof is a ridge comb which extends into dragon heads projecting over the gables. These are inspired by Norwegian stave churches, but here they seem to be in a better mood than their forefathers. This dragon style is usually considered very Norwegian, but here, the proportions in the body of the building are clearly European, as was often the case with the "Swiss style" in the second half of the there 19th century. In keeping with the fashion of the day, there was a large, open veranda on the front facade facing the view, but it was enclosed with large glass panels at a relatively early date.

National romanticism, benevolent dragons and knickknacks

The hotel building was opened in 1895, and it was surrounded by a number of smaller cottages and villas, as were many so-called sanitariums where people could remain for long periods of time. In addition, there was a farm with its accompanying buildings. Some of these smaller buildings also were in the dragon style, inspired by old Norwegian wooden buildings, but without dragon decoration. There were plans to move older buildings from the district up to the area around the hotel, but this seems to have been limited to a fine two-story storehouse, which was moved early on. A new storehouse, built in the 1890's right across from the hotel, features more decoration.

Architect Hjalmar Welhaven (1850-1922) designed the hotel and probably some of the smaller buildings. He was palace administrator for King Oscar II and had designed summer villas for the court at Bygdøy (by Oslo) in the 1870's, and he presented plans for a large summer house for the king there, too. All had the characteristics of national romanticism, with unpaneled log walls or dragon decor on the gable apexes, and were very early examples of the style.

The finances of the firm which built Tuddal Mountain Hotel were not the best, so the buildings are less ornate than many others in this special style. But the main building is very well preserved in its original state. Through the years, it has acquired only smaller additions at one end – a smoking room and an office from the end of the 1920's. The so-called sun room and the library were built over the previous addition in 1938, in a style typical of the time, with a flat roof and a long band of windows across the facade. In 1995-1996, the flat roof was harmonized with the original building through an extension of the large main roof.

Just inside the main entrance is a hall which has been made into a monumental room with two free-standing columns and two symmetrical staircases up to the second floor. From there, one can see through the lounge and out over the landscape. For the most part, the unpainted log walls, with 100 years of patina, characterize the interiors in the lounges and in the guest bedrooms. By contrast, the smoking room has plywood paneling, which was modern at the end of the 1920's, but even this veneer looks like newly scrubbed wood.

The hotel features an unusually large collection of antiques and old furnishings from different periods. Some of the pieces were new when the hotel was built, but most were collected by Gudrun Gurholt.

From the beginning, Tuddal had an open veranda facing the view. Over the years, it has been integrated into the dining room and lounge inside.
Photograph: Gullik Rua at the end of the 1890's.

These include sitting groups from the last century and a large number of pieces in Neo-Baroque and Pseudo-Rococo from the beginning of this century, which have acquired the patina only possible through long years of use.

The large collection of Norwegian rustic furniture is worth mentioning, especially the many old tapestries, coverlets and wool drapes. Some are woven in traditional checkerboard and star patterns, while others have some aspects of Art Nouveau combined with traditional shapes from around the turn of the century. Telemark style rosepainting can be seen on doors and artifacts all around the hotel. The most recent rosepainting dates from the beginning of the 1950's,

when a local painter spent the winter in the building. The greatest treasure is the hollowed log boat which was found nearby, said to be about 2000 years old.

Tradition is still respected at Tuddal Mountain Hotel. After a period when it was leased out, the hotel has been reborn in its former beauty. Room standards have been raised through installation of small baths, while the rooms themselves have retained their traditional feel, with furnishings which are not necessarily luxurious, but which create a mood and continue a tradition. In some rooms, the furnishings are the same as they always have been.

In connection with the extension of the roof in 1995-1996, some new, smaller verandas were built with details selected from the original building. Work done today has to take into consideration guests' demands for comfort as well as fire regulations, so emphasis has been placed on finding solutions which retain the original interiors as much as possible. Instead of installing a sprinkler system which would have compromised the old interior, the owners chose to close off the attic rooms and accept the loss of capacity. Rather than lowering the ceilings in the first floor, the floors in the guest rooms above have been raised to hide new plumbing. Small details, such as new electrical wiring in well-chosen colors, are hardly noticeable. The lost guest capacity is now being gained by renovating the older annexes, and a new annex in the hotel's original style and materials is in the planning stage.

Among larger hotels from the period around 1900, Tuddal Mountain Hotel is probably the best preserved, if both exterior and interior are evaluated together. The excellent collection of antiques and old furniture contributes to the hotel's unique ambiance and makes even a stroll through the long hotel corridor a journey of discovery.

1. Holmenkollen Hotel, 25 x 43 cm (10 x 17 in)

2. Bårdshaug Herregård, 25 x 43 cm (10 x 17 in)

3. Kvikne's Hotel, 24 x 33 cm (9.5 x 13 in)

4. Husum Hotell, 24 x 33 cm (9.5 x 13 in)

5. Utne Hotel, 24 x 33 cm (9.5 x 13 in)

6. Hotel Dalen, 24 x 33 cm (9.5 x 13 in)

Memories of a Journey

On journeys, the unforeseen happens.
Nature is overwhelming
hospitality grand
and dreams clear:

Holmenkollen a winter evening,
Fjærland a spring morning,
Solvorn with mountains so near,
Utne with apples and cider and
Balestrand a quiet summer morning
with poppies on the veranda.

The mystical night
in Dalen in Telemark
With the sound of waterfalls and river,
Lærdal's white gem, Husum.
And Bårdshaug, a meeting of Trønder
longhouse and European architecture.

Kjell Thorjussen is one of our most popular graphic artists. He is especially known for his atmospheric pictures of houses in beautiful landscapes.

In the lithographic technique used here, the motif is first drawn on stone blocks, and color is applied later. Then the motif is transferred to paper by means of a special technique. In all, 5-7 colors are printed on top of one another. These interact and make the finished expression. Each picture is an independent work of art, numbered and signed by the artist. The pictures are made in editions of only 150.

Kjell Thorjussen (b. 1942) received his education at the National School of Trade and Applied Art and the National Academy of Fine Arts. He has participated in the National Autumn Exhibition since 1973, a long list of group exhibitions in Norway and abroad, along with one-man-shows at the Artists' Association in Oslo and in many other cities in Norway. His works are in the collections of the National Gallery, the Norwegian Cultural Council and the Swedish State Council for the Arts, and others.

7. Hotel Mundal, 39 x 21 cm (15.5 x 8.5)

8. Hotell Walaker, 39 x 21 cm (15.5 x 8.5)

All pictures are for sale and can be ordered from
KOM Forlag, Vågeveien 10, 6500 Kristiansund
Telephone: (47) 71 67 83 00, Telefax: (47) 71 67 83 60

Pictures 1–2: NOK 1100, pictures 3–8: NOK 950
A 3% charge is added to the price of each picture to benefit the Artists' Aid Fund.